# MARISA MOMENTS:
## BEGIN <u>YOUR</u> JOURNEY

## About the Author

Marisa Ikpoh is a wife, the mother of two beautiful daughters, an intuitive-sensitive, clairvoyant and medium. She has chosen to accept life's many perceived obstacles with a positive outlook and is sharing her moments through transparency with the intention of spreading hope and eliciting change on a global scale. She has been published with such humanitarian outlets as *The Master Shift* and *25 Ways to Gain Emotional Strength*. She has received testimony from numerous individuals and public figures on the positive effects of her inspirational messages.

Please visit her online at www.MarisaMoments.com

# MARISA MOMENTS: BEGIN YOUR JOURNEY

by M. Ikpoh

The Christopher Isaac Society
Chicago, Illinois

*Marisa Moments: Begin YOUR Journey* ©2014 by Marisa Ikpoh (CreateSpace Indie Publishing). All rights reserved. No part of this book may be used or reproduced in any manner whatsoever, including Internet usage, without written permission from The Christopher Isaac Society or Marisa Ikpoh, except in the case of brief quotations embodied in critical articles and reviews.

First Edition
First Printing, 2014

Book design by Marisa Ikpoh
Cover Images: CreateSpace
Editor: Christopher Ikpoh
Editor: Sean Isaac Lee

ISBN-13: 978-1500377229
ISBN-10: 1500377228

## To Write to the Author

If you wish to contact the author or would like further information on the book and its contents, please write to the author by emailing: Marisa@marisamoments.com. The author appreciates hearing from you and receiving feedback on how this book has helped you and how you are making a difference in this world. We cannot guarantee that every message sent to the author will be answered, but best efforts will be taken to return all correspondence.

To

My totally tubular family…

Chris, my amazing hubbykins (and editor); whom I love to the moon and back!

Vanessa, my empathically compassionate, Indigo Child, daughter

Jasmine, my energetically fearless flower-child, daughter

My mama and my sister. [MP & SW]

And all else that have, and continue to inspire and motivate the journey.

You ALL mean the worlds to me!!!!!!!

## **Early Reader Testimonials**

*"The book is so compelling... The stories truly show that we can always learn a lesson in any life experience that can impact our lives in a positive way as long as we are open to the change. Very inspiring."*
–M. Rodriguez

*"I ABSOLUTELY see where you're going with your awesome, highly ambitious 1st book. You should be VERY proud, well done!"*
–S. Lee

*"I love the feel of it. Not super heavy on the 'perform these exercises in order to promote growth', just, here is my story, I hope it can in some way help you. !!"*
–M. Negron-Schilling (*Abundance Abounds Antiques*)

"...Because the world won't change until YOU do..."
-MDI

# Table of Contents

| | | |
|---|---|---|
| I. | WHY THIS? WHY NOW? | 12 |
| II. | PAYING ATTENTION | |
| | The Story – Reality | 17 |
| |     Escape | 20 |
| |     Signs | 21 |
| III. | NO COINCIDENCES | |
| | The Story – The Catalyst of Change | 24 |
| |     Hiding When I need to Seek | 30 |
| |     Battles | 31 |
| |     No Coincidences | 33 |
| IV. | EMOTIONAL TRIGGERS | |
| | The Story – Urgent Rumbles | 36 |
| |     Perception | 40 |
| |     Let go for real | 42 |
| V. | 'GOOD' VS. 'BAD' | |
| | The Story – The White Witch | 46 |
| |     Bad Habits | 53 |
| |     Complain versus Vent | 56 |
| |     Yelling | 58 |
| |     Let him use you | 59 |
| VI. | HARDSHIPS & STRUGGLES IN LIFE | |
| | The Story – The Shark Attack | 63 |
| |     Attacks | 69 |
| |     Struggles | 72 |

## VII. STANDING IN THE GAP

| | |
|---|---|
| The Story – No Passes | 76 |
| Mistake your Kindness | 84 |
| Stand Up! | 86 |
| Guard your Words | 88 |

## VIII. OVERCOMING THE ENEMY AGAINST ALL ODDS

| | |
|---|---|
| The Story – Dangerous Creatures | 92 |
| Weary but Hopeful | 98 |
| Answers | 100 |
| Growth | 102 |
| Calling the Enemy's Bluff | 103 |

## IX. THE RELEASE

| | |
|---|---|
| The Story – Over the Edge | 106 |
| Let it go | 108 |
| Releasing Labels | 110 |
| Let it go II | 112 |

## X. STEP OUTSIDE OF YOUR COMFORT ZONE

| | |
|---|---|
| The Story – Visions | 115 |
| I can only be me | 120 |
| A Lucid Dream | 123 |
| My Truths | 125 |

## XI. REBUILDING AND MOVING FORWARD

| | |
|---|---|
| The Story – Under Construction | 129 |
| Get Grounded | 136 |
| Sync your Steps | 137 |
| Moving Ahead | 140 |

XII.  THE SEDUCTION

    The Story – Lured by Darkness     142
            Overruled     145
            Invisible Attacks     147
            Rejection     148
            Demons     150
            Embracing the Shadows     152

XIII.  HOW FAR WE'VE COME

    A Glance over the Shoulder     156

## Chapter I: WHY THIS? WHY NOW?

I used to have a "glass half empty, question everything, believe nothing" outlook on life. Yet, I always felt as if there was something missing within myself. I lived most of my life in a bubble of cynicism and general disdain for anything that was, in my opinion, of no consequence to me. I could truly care less about the feelings of others and went about my life as I saw fit, regardless of the impact my actions had. It is only now that I recognize most of my actions were rooted in self-sabotage. I never thought myself deserving of true happiness, so why would I invest in the happiness of those around me? I was a walking/talking, self-fulfilling prophecy of negativity and sorrow. I was creating my own dark reality and then blaming others for its existence.

It was only after a series of unfortunate events including the passing of a great friend's father-in-law, a horrific mass shooting in an elementary school and a terrorist attack at a marathon, that I found myself waking up to the reality I actively tried to ignore. My heart was touched in such a way that I began to literally feel the pain of others. Then, I began receiving visions, dreams, of things that I had no logical reason to know. My mind was being opened to receive more than I ever dreamed possible. It was as if I was finally being awakened from the slumber that began when I was a teen. I was changing as an individual and knew that I had only one option - acceptance.

The beauty I am now uncovering, through self-discovery and by following the path towards internal peace, is what carries me through the ebb and flow of my life experiences. I am an intuitive, empath, clairvoyant and a medium; amongst other things. Yet, these things do not define me. They simply allow me to bridge the gap as it relates to my ongoing journey and encourage others on their path towards a more positive existence. My gifts simply allow me to broaden my reach, to touch the hearts of many that I might not have been able to meet otherwise. I now know, and accept, that it is by grace that I've made it this far with the blessings the universe has bestowed. Furthermore, I know it is by grace that I will continue towards the beautiful destiny bequeathed to me before I ever met the Earth.

I am greatly aware that we all have different journeys to our various destinies. However, if we don't take steps towards understanding and making peace within ourselves, we will not be able to make the even grander steps toward affecting change. This is why I share 'Marisa Moments' with you. I offer my moments with full transparency and love because I recognize that I am not alone in the daily struggles of life. If I can share my inner light enough to ignite a spark of encouragement, change, or growth within even one other soul, I am fulfilled.

This isn't an egocentric journey. It is one of purity and positivity. I accept that my purpose is not to change minds. My purpose is to awaken those that are ready to unplug from the matrix and truly see themselves and the world around them for what it really is, and what it could be.

Change is a process that does not occur overnight. It requires work and diligence on our part. There are many different stages to accepting and creating change that lasts. Whether you aim to shift your perceptions, alter the way you 'deal' with the things you encounter, enhance your ability to accept opinions that differ from your own, or receive enlightenment from a higher plane, you must be willing to put forth the effort to receive results.

In the coming chapters, I will share with you various short stories that are focused on the reality in which we all exist. Some may shock you, make you laugh or anxious. They all serve the common purpose of offering lessons and even reality checks, though. I will focus on the six stages of change -- denial, contemplation, preparation, action, living and relapse -- as they relate to my personal journey. The paradigm is sometimes obscure and at other times obvious in everyday life. Later these stories are grounded and made even clearer through connections to my real-life experiences and journal entries. I invite you into my world with hopes that these glimpses will resonate with you, and confirm that you are not alone in any of your struggles, for it is in these struggles that we can find our true strength. Once you resolve to change your perspective and embrace positivity, you will be amazed at the wonder that comes your way. Will today be the day you decide to "be the change you wish to see in the world"?

## Chapter II: PAYING ATTENTION

### REALITY

I doubted everything in the past. If you would have told me that the sky was blue, I would chuckle as I looked up to confirm the information. To say I was 'cynical' would be an understatement. Good and bad only existed as I saw fit, and the concepts of change and/or positivity were laughable at best.

I would tell myself, "Oh really, you want to be a beacon of light? I think you'd have a better chance at morphing into a piece of bacon. I mean how could one person make a difference in this world?" I told myself we are hopeless people stuck in our selfish ways of being. There are a small percentage of people that have obscene wealth, whilst the remaining ninety-nine percent of the world struggle just to make ends meet. I figured if we really wanted to address the imbalance, we would look towards making use of sustainable natural resources and shift towards a basic redistribution of wealth.

The reality is people believe, "Oh, but wait… you can't make as much money as I do if I have to work harder. And you certainly can't take money out of my pocket if I was the one that earned it." There are people making millions of dollars to play a sport and yet, we have educators earning pennies in comparison. I know, the teachers are only working to shape young minds. Why would they deserve a salary that would even compare to that of a professional athlete? Then, we wonder why underprivileged youth focus more on lay-ups than literacy.

Our priorities are so out of whack; we scurry past the homeless without a second thought, en route to purchase our branded coffee. We dismiss the struggles of our neighbor in the same manner that we throw out the trash. Our behavior indicating thoughts of, "We don't need them, so who cares? If I don't have to see it or be impacted by it directly, I don't care." Think about it, we have become so desensitized to real struggle and pain yet we are entertained by it on television as a means of escape.

Wait, what am I yammering on about? Everything is fine. The world is running like a well-oiled machine and we all live in the land of plenty and opportunity. There is nothing to worry about, so excuse me as I browse the internet on my tablet, enjoy a fresh brewed cup of decadence and fast-forward through my DVR'd reality television shows. I won't even <u>think</u> about lifting a finger until the universe tells me it's time.

Oh, but wait. It has. I guess I wasn't paying attention.

## <u>Behind the Story</u>

Doubt is a natural part of life and it is even more ingrained in those of us that take a cynical stance on everything that crosses our path. The key is to find balance within that doubt. Encourage questions and allow yourself, and others, to forever evolve based on new knowledge. However, we must be careful not to cross the fine line of complete skepticism.

## Journal Entry: "Escape"

As I head home on the bus, I am drawn to the sight of a tiny insect flying in circles against the window. It is clearly trying to return to the outside world from which it found itself abruptly removed. I find it interesting how this relates to a definitive part of my life.

This tiny creature sees its home through the window and charges it with all its might. It remains diligent and focused on its task, and seems fervent on the notion of freedom and change from the atmosphere in which it found itself confined. With each flight towards the light, it is met by the cold feeling of the glass in front of its face. Though mocked by the notion of independence, it doesn't give up. But why? I'm struggling to see the point of frivolous attempts to escape. It's clearly in denial about its situation and reality. ♥

*Journal Entry: "Signs"*

Throughout life I have experienced many ups and downs. I've had extended periods of happiness and extremely extended periods of despair, depression and disappointment. What I failed to do during these times of trial, was hold strong to my faith. (I'm not perfect.) I've asked, "Why me?" and gone as far as wanting to completely give up because, well, what was the point? At least that was how I saw it.

During this journey, I have continued with life's many ups-and-downs with one exception: my outlook. I now choose to see things in a more positive light, even when it seems near impossible.

I am realizing that signs are truly everywhere, and I choose to see them as gifts from above to help guide us through this thing called life. The way I see it, there is no such thing as coincidence, we need only but pay attention to the world around us for cues from our predestined paths. ♥

## What does it all mean?

Are you starting to understand the flow of change? You see, we all have moments of doubt and utter despair. How could we not? We are human. However, it is what we choose to do in these moments that ultimately make a difference in the instances to come. I don't mean to imply that this is a simple journey, because it is certainly not for the faint of heart. What you choose to do once you start recognizing that change is necessary; is what can make all the difference in your world.

Just keep in mind that everything happening in this life, happens for a reason. I completely understand that this is an incredibly difficult pill to swallow when it comes to the *bad* times. However once you start training your mind and eyes to see beyond the veil of typical understanding, it will become easier to embrace the fact that there are no coincidences. Open your mind towards the possibilities, and then allow the universe to guide your steps.

## Chapter III: NO COINCIDENCES

### THE CATALYST OF CHANGE

Somehow I found myself walking down what appeared to be an abandoned road. There were power plants on both sides of the road that were emitting huge clouds of gray and black smoke into the air. Suddenly, a man appears behind me, walking in-step with every movement that I make. I feel uneasy by his sudden appearance, but I am comforted by the space between us, as this provides an unspoken means of escape. Just as I am in the midst of thoughts of an escape plan, another man appears and charges after the first. He has a guitar in his hands and fire in his eyes.

My body and mind are filled with the notion of looming disaster. I am frozen by the shock of what I foresee to be a gruesome attack of unknown anger. Just as I realize what is about to take place, my voice escapes my lips in a manner that seems foreign to my person. Anguish, fear and disbelief well-up and spill out.

"NOOO.... STOOOOOPPPPPPP!!!!!!" are the only two words I can muster the courage to say. Yet, my words fall on deaf ears. Neither man seems to even notice my presence. The fight begins with the sound of the guitar being smashed over the head of the other man. It is a brutal attack with no sign of relief. I run over, trying desperately to scream reality back into their hearts and minds, but I am too late. The deep crimson colors mixed with spongy white and pink pieces of flesh are proof positive that this man's end is certain.

Then, as if arising from the dust in the wind, people began to appear behind the fences that keep the workers contained in the plants, while preventing outsiders from gaining access. These people are modern day slaves, held captive by their masters that peddle pollution to the masses. I am entranced by their presence and more so by the fact that they don't seem to notice that I am there. They raise their voices in protest against one another, based on which side of the road they stand. It's an all-out war based on nothing more than physical proximity.

One woman screams to the guitar wielding man, "It's the same thing day-after-day. Why must you always kill him?!"

I begin to weep openly at the sight of a seemingly unavoidable and senseless death. It is only through this raw display of heartfelt emotion that, it appears, for the first time they notice my presence. They turn towards me simultaneously, and in an instant look at each other. They allowed their brows of fury to relax and truly looked at one another. Finally, they were open to receiving the truth about themselves and their surroundings. A long forgotten truth was ready to be rediscovered.

The truth was knowing, that in reality, they were all the same. They realized that what they were fighting for was nothing more than an illusion created to separate them from one another. They were actually brothers and sisters that had long forgotten their connection. Even the factories for which they toiled were identical to one another, with the exception of their physical location; they were separated by a chain-link fence to perpetuate the notion of divide. The illusion worked perfectly, pitting brother against brother and sister against sister. The division served to promote hatred and discord, the ensuing violence became a distraction from the truth.

It was in this same moment that the collective recognized that they had been pawns in a world of indentured servitude, caught in a never ending loop of slaving to live and living to be enslaved. Each passing day offered nothing more than indifference towards universal struggle, and emotional abuse created by the very system they were fighting to protect. The system did not care to provide security, instead it kept its servants on a short leash of mandatory employment. The rules of engagement were mindless work or lay-offs and dismissals. The master lived in the clouds looking down upon those that broke their backs to unwittingly sustain the utopia of another. They were nameless and faceless pawns used to ensure the wealth of another regardless of the blood, sweat and tears shed in the process.

I could see the people slowly beginning to wake-up with each tear that I shed. I continued to weep openly until I had no more tears. In that moment I approached the man who, minutes before, I witnessed kill another, and gave him a hug. I didn't hug him as a means of support for his violent actions. No, I hugged him as an acknowledgement of the trap he had now found himself in. One single action of exhausted faith, ended the life of his brother, and it was he alone that was now waking up from the very illusion which fed his anger. He was now faced with the consequences of his slumber. It served neither as excuse nor as solace, for his brother lay slain in the road of division.

The only certainty was in knowing something needed to change, and this moment was the catalyst for that change to begin.

## Behind the Story

Generally, I would follow this story with a lesson. However, in the beginning I believe we must come to our own conclusions if we are truly to find our own way along this journey to a greater destiny. Therefore, instead I will simply open the blinds to reveal the truths in my soul. The workers in the aforementioned story are not alone in their slumber, for I too struggle with hitting the proverbial snooze button, when in reality I should be awake. Contemplation can often serve as a lesson in itself. We just need to be willing to consider.

03/15/15

How do you relate to this story? Do you consider yourself a worker or the hidden boss? Are you running into the fight, cheering it on? Or, are you calling for the proverbial cease fire?

*Right now I am running into the fight... we need help at work & keep asking so now quitting... vessel of change?*

*Journal Entry: "Hiding when I need to Seek"*

Over-thinking has always been the name of my game. I say something or type something and wonder if I should have rephrased my words so that I can avoid sounding aggressive or uncaring. I even try to smile as I type a message in the hopes that the warmth of my words can be felt when they are read. I don't necessarily see this as a character *flaw*. It just means that I care...a lot.

This caring can lead to hurt. The problem isn't that I care, but that my over thinking often causes me to pull back when reality screams for me to push forward. The lesson of my inaction is simple: I must hold firm to my truth no matter the consequences. I can't avoid representing HIS words for fear of rejection. True enough, some may disregard what I attempt to say, but my focus should not be obscured by darkness or dejection. I must keep my eyes on the light and trust that those meant to listen and join. WILL.

Today, I recognize that I must stop hiding when I need to seek. My light shines for all to see, and my edict is to encourage change in the hearts and actions of those that are willing. This doesn't mean that I don't care about the ones that choose another path. It means that I aim to awaken those that are tired of the slumber.

So, are you ready to wake-up? ♥

### Journal Entry: "Battles"

I often get so enthralled in the notion of encouraging positive change that I lose touch with the harsh reality of having to stand my ground when the time is right. This journey has caused many rude awakenings, and I have been faced with the choice of letting things go, accepting my lessons, shifting my perceptions to reflect strength and positivity, etc. Yet, on this day, I am forced to weigh in on having to put on a proverbial suit of armor and fight for the light.

Of course the notions of good/bad and right/wrong are all based on individual perceptions. However, my battles of late are ones that seek balance and harmony. You see, I'm in a moment of great growth. I can feel it in my soul and I am getting better at recognizing this growth because it is in these times of advancement that I am most likely to be tested. I am open to receiving light, but I must be aware that my openness also makes me a prime target for darkness. My perceptions, which were once trained on truth, shift to paranoia and my sensitivities are put on a razor's edge. Thing of it is, darkness will play on <u>anything</u> that it perceives to be a path to our souls. Therefore, in these times of growth, I must be vigilant against reacting on assumptions that are based on dark subliminal messages rooted in lies. I will stand my ground and 'fight' by counteracting the darkness with the great light within my being.

I will not stand for attacks against myself or those that I love. I will cast out anything that tries to tear at my core and create self-doubt. Nothing is more important than my foundation, my <u>true</u> family. For myself and them I will put on my suit of armor and blind the enemy with the brilliance within my soul. I <u>AM</u> a good soul and a soldier of HIS will. No weapons formed against me shall prosper; not mental, physical or emotional.

Begin Your Journey / 33

==Today, I remind myself that I will not only win the battles, but I will also win the war when it comes to the change I wish to see.== This does not mean welcoming violence. It speaks to preparing for *battle* with love and light. ♥

### Journal Entry: "No Coincidences"

One thing I've noticed lately is that everything in my life has been connected. Whether it's something on TV that touches on a conversation I had a few days prior, a discussion that taps into recent experiences, or an action that reinforces a thought. I believe that there truly are no coincidences in life.

My blessing lately has been in being able to recognize the links between what I would have considered just everyday occurrences. ==This recognition though, comes with responsibility.== Nothing severe. ==It simply requires acknowledgement and acceptance.== It is truly my blessing, and if you are willing to be aware of your surroundings, it can be your blessing too!

The moment you begin to connect the dots in life, you will realize without a doubt that you are precisely where you are meant to be. All the hardships, the joys, the sorrows, the disappointments, the triumphs, etc, everything was for a reason, and those moments (good and bad) were all placed on your path to lead you to your destiny. Moreover, those events and trials not only test but strengthen, for had you not experienced the darkness, you would not truly understand how to appreciate the light.

Embrace your destiny, but don't use it as an excuse to remain in a lie. Yes, everything happens for a reason. On the other hand, remaining where you know you shouldn't be will create a detour on your path. Keep moving forward, look for the links in life, and be willing to accept reality and the lessons it provides. ♥

~*~*~*~

## What does it all mean?

We must pay attention if we choose to travel this path. No two paths are alike. Nevertheless, I have found that being able to relate to the journey of another can serve as a great means of comfort. You see, even the fact that you are reading these words right now is no coincidence. This book, this information, this journey will all serve a higher purpose in the bigger picture. Still, as I've illustrated in the personal journal moments before, there is much to this path. My aim is to cultivate, welcome and embrace positive change for myself, and in-turn, the world around me. In order to do so, we must remain honest with ourselves and recognize that sometimes we create moments of struggle by not paying attention to our own emotional triggers. Let us therefore take a closer look at what these triggers can look like, by taking a step towards change. Let's move towards preparation.

Chapter IV: EMOTIONAL TRIGGERS

URGENT RUMBLES

When I ride the bus past a certain gas station I am always reminded of the day I had stomach issues that led me to alter my plans and act swiftly to find relief from the battle in my gut. I still had about six stops to go before getting to my destination, but I knew I couldn't tolerate another road bump or red light. I remember walking with great urgency into the gas station near the bus stop. As I power walked through the doors you could only imagine my frustration seeing the clerk busy with another customer. In my mind, my only option was to wait patiently while the customer before me picked his perfect pack of smokes. I prayed silently as the sweat threatened to drop from my brow, hoping that no one would suspect the physical discomfort I was suffering.

I shifted my weight from leg to leg and looked around the establishment to distract my mind with anything I could see or read. Well, it just so happened that my 'distraction' revealed a well hidden note put up by management indicating that the restroom was 'Out Of Order'. Yikes and awesome! I immediately asked the clerk, completely disregarding the customer he was still helping, if he knew of the nearest restroom. He directed me to a dive restaurant on a catty corner two blocks from where I currently stood. If it weren't for the two stoplights between me and the restaurant, I might've actually considered it. After all, desperate times call for desperate measures, so although I sized the place up to be a 'four-layer toilet cover' location, I definitely would have gone there. After all, it wasn't the most unsanitary place I'd ever encountered on urgent business.

However, there was no way on this green Earth that my bowels could make it that far! I had to act quickly; otherwise, I would need reinforcements (I'm talking pants, not people). So I exited as quickly as I entered and walked to the next open building. It was one of those pop-up cell phone stores that didn't require a contract to take your money. Well, since my instincts told me that there was no public restroom I used the oldest trick in the book...

"Excuse me, ma'am. I'm pregnant and REALLY have to go to the restroom. May I use yours?"

It just so happened that the woman -- and only employee on grounds -- was busy with a phone call so she barely gave me a second glance as she walked me through a construction area leading to a restroom. In my mind, I was thanking all things holy for this woman's kindness, but wanted to literally shove her out of the way to get some relief. There I was, throwing my backpack to the floor with my coat immediately following. There was no time to inspect for cleanliness. I had a mission.

Click* Click*

Click\* Click\* Click\* Click\* Click\* Click\*

"Really?! The light doesn't work? This is super. Whelp, beggars can't be choosy."

Do you know that I left the door cracked open as if I were at home and commenced to find relief? Hey, a gal's got to do what a gal's got to do!

## Behind the Story

I tell you this story not to shock you, because we have all been there a time or two. I share this because I think of this moment, every time I pass that gas station, and I can't help but smile. The memory and urgency all comes rushing back, including thoughts of my panicked call to my husband explaining that he was still going to have to love me post-explosion (in the off chance that I didn't make it in time). This moment has turned into a trigger that elicits laughter. See where I'm going with this?

Fact is, we all have emotional triggers. Some are perceived as good, while others are perceived as bad. We need only alter our viewpoints in order to have a different poignant response. After all, it's not always about what happened as much as how we view and perceive the events.

### Journal Entry: "Perception"

Here's what I know: not everyday is filled with sunshine and daffodils. However, I choose to see things from a positive perspective to get through the rough times and to truly enjoy the good times. I've received signs that negativity is haunting my current existence, but I recognize that this is the enemy's work. I also understand that I may, subconsciously, be taking strides towards self-sabotage for fear of success. So every time there is an action that pushes me down, I must choose to push back with the strength that I have been blessed with. I meet resistance, real and perceived, with the refusal to be held down!

I'm not saying this to assert my approach on others. I'm sharing this because we all have the choice to shift our perception to create a kinder reality. I'm not suggesting that we live in a bubble; casting out all reality while skipping down the yellow brick road and sporting our rose colored glasses. To the contrary, I say we must acknowledge life and its experiences for what they are. Grant yourself permission to truly feel the moments (*good and bad*), without absorbing them into our existence. We should alter our ultimate view to sparingly filter out the negative that could lead to darkness and despair. It is imperative that we hold on to whatever positivity that moments in this life can lend. Express gratitude openly and accept that we deserve nothing short of happiness. Take the lessons from your experiences and keep moving forward.

When I see signs and suggestions that indicate my existence is largely contingent on being dragged through the proverbial mud, I refuse to be discouraged. I own my role in everything that happens within my life and I am thankful for even the harshest lessons. I know without having been pushed by a negative force in a downward direction, I might not have exerted myself to oppose that force. Consequently, I would not have ended up living in clarity, love and light.

I smile in the face of the enemy and call him a bold-faced liar. My perception is one of positivity and with greatness by my side; no weapons formed against me shall prosper! I am beginning to own my choices and, therefore, preparing to invoke change. ♥

Journal Entry: "Let go for Real"

I had a vision that I was gifted a moment of clarity before imminent disaster struck. This moment told me to be still, although there would be devastation around me. It showed me that although the results would be of epic proportions, I and those immediately around me would escape all consequence if I fought all instincts to run, and instead held my ground. Then, the explosion occurred. It brought debris flying at me and all around me. Yet, I remained still while praying with all my might and trusting that HIS word would never lead me to my own detriment. I can't lie to you, I wanted to run and head for the hills. Instead, I stood firm.

After the flames died, there was mass destruction all around. Yet, I felt so extremely blessed. I had been taken through the storms but there I stood with my family. We had made it through; we were survivors of our circumstances. I didn't look at things as them having happened to me. I instead re-framed my perceptions and saw that every moment of this event strengthened me. I stood in my faith and it brought us through.

Of course the lesson in this is very clear. However, I recognize that the lessons in any moment are often more than the naked eye chooses to embrace. So, from the images I have been graciously shown, my heart recognizes and acknowledges how I've been holding on to many questions and so much pain. I wonder, *"Why?"* time-after-time, and I am never met with the response that I deem to be acceptable.

> *I have to take pause to chuckle at myself in this moment. Isn't it funny how we have a tendency to ask questions, but if we don't receive the answer that we were expecting or want, we keep looking for further answers?! I know it's not just me. But, I digress.*

Begin Your Journey / 44

*This is where you↲*

The point is this. In this dream, I had to let go of my usual response of flight in order to survive the impact of what was to take place around me. I had to be still and trust that things would be OK. I couldn't just say that I had let go while keeping a firm hold in my heart. I was given the test of a moment that screamed for me to trigger my customary responses of escape. Instead I had to release and trust my heart through actions, not just words. Now I know that I must follow suit. I need to accept the answers I receive while moving forward without hesitation, instead of hoping that answers will change to suit my desires.

Yes, sometimes we must fight for what is meant for us, but I find real strength in knowing exactly when to simply let go. Comfort can be found even in the harshest of circumstances if we are able to free ourselves of what we are used to, and are willing to grasp that which we usually ignore. When we let go, we allow ourselves room for growth. I encourage you to pay attention to the signs around you. When they all point in one direction, you should probably consider following the signs. Perhaps this is your notice that it's time to prepare yourself to let go. ♥

~*~*~*~

## What does it all mean?

When we pay close attention to ourselves and the typical responses we have to any given situation, we take a step closer to internal peace. I don't pretend to know myself inside and out, because the more I learn, the more I grow and change. However, as is the case with a growing child, we shouldn't stop paying attention and marking new stages of change simply because we will not be the same in the next moments. Instead, I support mile markers as beautiful reminders of our growth, understanding that individual notions of progress will vary.

Bear in mind, we shouldn't be quick to label our journey, ourselves, or another because just as everyone's triggers vary from soul-to-soul, perceptions of *good* or *bad* are completely in the eye of the beholder. Labels are a convenient box that others can put you in, a means of limiting the possibilities that we all possess within ourselves. It's time to step outside the box and just be.

## Chapter V: 'GOOD' VS. 'BAD'

### THE WHITE WITCH

Years ago we went on a combined family vacation. This was not the norm, but it was completely cozy. The cabin was very rustic, which by my own accounts was never anything I would typically find myself drawn to. Stain glass windows lined the walls just below the dark- natural wooden beams that framed the ceiling. It felt as if the entire place was carved out of a tree, with a few modern additions to remove the mystery behind its true location. We were in the midst of all that Mother Nature had left. It was as close to nature as any of us could come with access to all the general conveniences we had grown accustomed. My eyes roamed from floor to ceiling, taking in as many of the natural details as possible. I was in awe of the natural beauty surrounding us. The medieval qualities served to make the location all the more appealing to the curious mind. One could imagine the rich history that befell every inch of the single room in which I stood, let alone the entire resort.

We didn't even have the opportunity to unpack or make ourselves comfortable with our new surrounding, when all residents were urgently called to gather in the main hall. As we walked into the room, I glanced around for any indication of what was taking place. I wondered, was this a part of the shtick for this place? Did my husband sign us up for some sort of 'themed vacation'? No one seemed to know what was happening, and I was growing slightly impatient.

Just as I began to shift my weight with anticipation, a woman dressed in a flowing white gown appeared. I was instantly mesmerized by her. She seemed to have such a glow around her. It was as if she floated in on white mist. She spoke softly but clearly enough to be understood. She warned of bad forces coming to try to take over. She said that we needed to remain resolute in our convictions; otherwise, we too risked being taken over by these dark forces.

Just as she finished her speech, I noticed that she herself started to change. Her eyes appeared to sink into her skull. Her features became darker, and her dress started to turn black. I looked around to make sure that I was not the only one witnessing these incredible events. Amazingly enough, the other residents were speaking amongst themselves. They had heard the announcement but could not see the metamorphosis taking place. I was stunned that no one seemed to notice that not only did the woman completely change, but her transformation appeared to be changing all that was good within her, to evil. She apologized to me as she was continuing to change, saying she knew this moment was inevitable, and then assured me that she would always remain good and true at the core of her existence. She told me that she didn't know if she would be strong enough to return to her former self once the change was complete, but urged me to remain steadfast and not allow myself to succumb to the darkness. She told me I must carry the good message forward to the world and allow my inner light to manifest in the absence of her own.

I was completely astonished. She was passing her torch of love and light to me to share with the world. Me! I had to take a moment to look away just to remind myself to breathe. My shoulders felt as if they would collapse from the weight of this new responsibility. Still, I knew that if I was given the mission, it was because I would be able to see it through.

Turning back to the newly transformed dark witch, in my heart I realized that she would become good again and find her way back to the light. However, I didn't know how long she would remain in her current form. Therefore, until then we were all prisoners, trapped by darkness and captive to her every whim. She named herself the ruler of all things and made no bones about using her dark magic against those that would even think about contradicting her directives. We moved, acted, spoke, ate, etc., as she directed. It was unnatural but necessary for our survival. Everyday, I would sneak glances into her eyes, eager for a glimmer of the white witch's return. I never lost hope and continued preaching goodness to those that remained. When they seemed to lose hope, I stepped forward to offer the energy necessary to keep them moving forward.

Exactly 3 months to the day of her original transformation into darkness -- during a makeshift carnival that the witch forced upon us in an evil effort to impose entertainment by way of her captives discomfort -- I glanced at the witch and saw the glimmer that I had longed for. The white witch was finally fighting her way back to the surface. With the opportunity before me, I ran to her and said... "By HIS grace, I compel you to come forward white witch! Together, we WILL defeat the enemy's hold and walk in love and light!"

With those words, the white witch returned and everything which turned evil and dark was now restored. The cabin had shifted from shadows and gloom, to its original state that welcomed nature and all beings of love.

...I Awaken...

The "witch transformation holiday" was just a dream. Oddly enough, I found myself in the living room of my cousin's house discussing my dream when her aunt walked out of a back room and began describing her dream. We had shared the exact same dream, but from different perspectives. She described the feeling of hopelessness and spoke of the petite, long haired woman that stood up for those that were at risk of losing all faith.

Was this really a dream? And if so, what are the chances of more than one person having the same dream from different vantage points? Did she recognize that the long-haired woman of which she spoke was me?

I didn't have much time to ponder my questions when, randomly enough, my cousin started speaking of her new pet tiger. Of course, I thought she was kidding, until she came walking out with this creature in her arms as if it were a baby. Initially, it appeared coy and completely harmless. However, I was uncomfortable with the idea of a wild animal being around my children, let alone being held as a domestic pet in anyone's home, least of all my cousin. I instructed my husband to pick up our youngest daughter for safe keeping, as it appeared the tiger had an infantile fascination with her. The animal kept trying to sniff and lick my child in a playful way, which made me uneasy. All I could think was if he was trying a sample portion before the full meal. There was no way this animal would come near either of my children, so I commanded him away in the strongest voice I could muster. At first, the command seemed effective, but the more I raised my voice and creased my brow, the more hostile the animal became. It appeared as though my assertion for dominance was now perceived by the animal to be an alpha challenge over territory. I was not ready to gamble with the life of my child, so we decided to leave and I advised my cousin to return the creature to its natural habitat in the wild, for the safety of herself, her children and the animal.

## Behind the Story

Good, bad, darkness, light; labels as they pertain to our journeys are only as powerful as we allow the terms to be. However, when we think of the words based on the general teachings most of us have grown accustom to, we must realize that they are all a necessary part of life. After all, without darkness we would never understand the true value of light and vise-versa. The key is to seek balance and understanding, not condemnation, for when we embrace who we are at our core and stand firm in protecting our foundation, we can never be overcome by the darkness. Yet, we must not stand so firmly that we forget our legs and become incapable of movement.

To understand and embrace our shadow selves does not mean to allow ourselves to be consumed by darkness. It requires that we acknowledge that we are all multidimensional beings; to renounce any part of ourselves is to deny self.

Journal Entry: "Bad Habits"

It is said that we, as a people, tend to notice the "annoying" habits of our neighbors because those habits are most likely a reflection of ourselves. I mention this because throughout this journey I have made it a point and I continue to work on staying humble. A part of this process requires strength in self reflection. This means that I not only have to look at my mirror image, but I need to study it. This is <u>no</u> easy task, let me tell ya.

Here's an example: I'm reading a book to my children for bedtime and I notice the premise of the story is literally, one character outdoing the other through metaphors to express their love for one another. (Yes, I'm sure I'm reading a bit too much into it, but that's neither here-nor-there.) I'm looking at this to determine how I can take away a lesson and in turn improve myself in accordance with my path. The more I read, the more I feel irritated by the one-up concept.

If you say that you ate one potato yesterday, I'm not going to one-up you and say I had two. Instead, I will let you have your story. I will be happy for your joy in sharing and will only insert my version when appropriate. Life isn't about tit-for-tat. It's about co-existing and uplifting. The contrary has always been a great source of irritation for me.

I say this not to show you that I'm obsessive (which I am), but to illustrate that there is literally a lesson in everything. We just need to open our eyes, hearts and souls to receive those lessons. Yes, I will continue to read the story to them (it's cute and they love it). However, I will take the opportunity to recognize this: the pointed dialogue that would normally ruffle my feathers instead offers a singular lesson that was intended for me to receive. That lesson being that my aggravation from the concept of one-upmanship is rooted in my tendency to turn things into a subconscious competition or to perceive others as doing so.

Point being: oftentimes we cannot just take things at face value. We must instead look beneath the surface to find our truth. We must not dismiss or judge the behavior of others, or turn a blind eye to that which we determine to be negative or dark. Instead, we must reflect on these perceptions to see how we can use the lessons to improve ourselves and possibly another (*if they are open to the suggestion*).

No one is perfect, but that doesn't mean we should stop trying.

♥

*Journal Entry: "Complain Versus Vent"*

Most mornings I like to start my day by sending random text messages to friends just to say "good morning" and to ask how they are. I do this because I want them to know that they are on my mind and because I truly care what's happening in their lives. However, I noticed that my response to the inevitable return inquiry towards my well being was often, "can't complain". This made me think about the concept of complaining in general. What is the point? It certainly doesn't get anything accomplished, and it doesn't even make the complainer feel better. So why do we do it?

Instead of complaining, I'll choose to vent. However, I know that I must do this with caution. The act of venting can easily cross over the line to complaining, and once again I will accomplish nothing.

To vent, in its literal sense, is to allow steam to escape in order to prevent combustion; once the steam has escaped, that venting should be done until the next required session. (Not Webster's... that's just my version.)

I was once told (by a very wise man) venting is fine if you say it once and then take action to make things better. I hold this very true. What is the point of repeatedly speaking on the same issue, when we refuse to claim our power by taking actions to affect change?

Today's task is to listen to you. Are you complaining or are you venting? Do you feel that one makes you find relief over the other? And in the face of either conversation, do you find comfort in speaking out on what you deem to be life's inequities? Or do you lead the charge to get out from under that which you feel serves as your oppressor?

I'm not aiming to assert my specific philosophies or ways of being on you. I just hope you begin to think about your current actions. If you discover that complaining does not help you, perhaps a change will do you good. ♥

*Change Agent*

Journal Entry: "Yelling"

Yelling is not a display of passion; it is simply an exertion of vocal cords. Truth can be whispered but still heard and echoed across an entire countryside. Yes, passion can oftentimes get the best of us. Nevertheless, when we know better, we must do better; or at least put forth an attempt. I mention this because we must always be cautious in our delivery. It is not out of respect for the other person as much as it is respect for self.

The next time someone provokes me to act out of character, I will try to take a moment to breathe and remain collected. The universe has the final say, so I will choose not to get stressed and try to assert my verbal version of forced karma by offering words that seek to play on the insecurities of another. Instead, when I'm wrong I will admit I am and apologize, and when I'm right, I will allow truth to speak for itself without gloating.

Standing up for good/righteousness does not have to manifest itself in an explosion of anger. It can be just as effective --if not more-- expressed in a calm, yet, articulate manner. I don't know about you, but I tend to get quiet so that I can hear when someone speaks softly. Besides, the notions of good and righteous vary from one person to another based on values and beliefs.

Think about it. You wouldn't have to oil a squeaky wheel if you constantly maintained the whole. Same as you wouldn't need to yell if you approached conversation from a place of respect and understanding. Therefore, today and moving forward, I will do my best to maintain my composure through all things that serve to challenge my peace. I will speak life into that which is good and refrain from dwelling on things that are not of, or from, love and light. Remember, we receive that which we emit. ♥

*we reap what we sow.*

Journal Entry: "Let HIM (God) use you"

I used to make excuses all the time. I would excuse the behavior of my friends, family and acquaintances by pointing fingers at the person next to them. I would cite physical or mental states as reasons behind actions. For example, "Oh, he/she is just tired". However, we are on the dawn of a new day. So today, I see the difference.

We go through different stages in our lives, some that are good and others, not so good, based on our individual perceptions. However, at every stage along the way we must acknowledge our own part in all acts. If you've done something wrong, you should own it and apologize whenever possible. Alternately, if you've done something positive, don't expect a ticker-tape parade. The good deed should be reward in itself.

I realize that some people allow themselves to be used as pawns of the enemy, for whatever reason. They behave in ways that serve to hinder their own personal growth and that of those around them without realizing how their words and actions affect others. Whereas others are fully aware of their Machiavellian ways and intentionally breathe life into manipulative behavior. This is where I ask, which are you?

Of course this is only posed if you are in fact carrying out negative deeds. Then again, I would like to think that you wouldn't purposely be doing 'bad' acts. Even so, I digress.

Look at your actions. Do they come from a *good* place? Are your intentions pure? Who is guiding your actions, and more importantly, your reactions? Don't be a puppet. Be an instrument of what is righteous; be led by your inner love and light. Do no harm unto others, whether it is physical or emotional. ♥

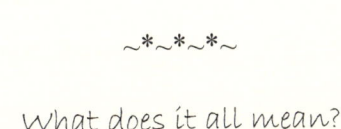

~*~*~*~

What does it all mean?

Perception more often than not reflects our individual realities, and labels function within the same confines. What I accept as *good* may be considered absolute torture to another. Yes, the lines can be blurred when it comes to receiving reality. However, that does not serve as permission to allow your actions to stray from what the heart deems as serving the greater good; without bringing harm to another. We must work diligently, learning to respect the differences of those around us.

Again, I don't assert that any of this is simple, but it is necessary for our evolution as individuals. Remember, the world will not change based on the actions of a group, but by the actions of individuals that work to coexist through light and love. There will always be struggles along the way, but we must trust in the knowledge that the *end* results will advance the survival of future generations.

*Work situation*

Chapter VI: HARDSHIPS & STRUGGLES IN LIFE

THE SHARK ATTACK

It was the perfect time for my girls and me to plan a getaway. After all, we had been working non-stop, and this was going to be some us time. Yes, a resort excursion with full amenities was exactly what the doctor ordered! As we drove down the road to our destination, a calm-comfortable silence settled in the vehicle. It was the first time in ages that any of us had a moment of uninterrupted peace, and we were going to drink it all in while we could.

Janessa had planned the trip, so it was fitting that she was the one behind the wheel taking us to our destination. Our convertible's top was down and the sun's warm rays were welcome on our skin, while the warm breeze kissed our cheeks. It was perfect, peaceful and serene.

I was lost in thought, arms stretched, eyes closed, and my head tilted back so my face could soak up the warmth of the sun. Suddenly, my concentration was broken by the sensation of our car turning off the main road we had been traveling on for over an hour. My eyes strained to adjust to the light of the sun even through my sunglasses. Slowly I began to focus on the lighthouse straight ahead.

Waves crashed with fury and huge sprays of water slicked the driveway that was encased by the cliff we found ourselves driving towards. Clearly, it was our destination, which made me uneasy; I even questioned Janessa's sanity in silence. Yet, she continued past the lighthouse and drove towards what appeared, to the naked eye, to be an enclosed cliff. In reality it was a man-made facade to shield the resort from public view. I still felt uneasy, but quieted my internal concerns and replaced them with outward signs of excitement. A smile flashed across my face and I gave a thumbs-up, as I tried not to kill the vibe of the adventure we were embarking on.

We went inside but were rushed through check-in and into our rooms because we were told that we had to be completely inside the resort before the tide, which was rising against the now closing faux-mountain facade. Once we were checked in there would be no early check-out, as Mother Nature would dictate the next time we would be allowed to meet 'the surface'. You see, the resort entrance was soon to be 10 feet under water, and therefore would 'ensure a good time', at least that's what the gentleman at check-in said. After we went to our rooms, we were told that the pool show and exercise areas were open, but we would need to change into our swimsuits within ten minutes in order to make it on time to the activities.

Once changed, we met in the hallway corridor and headed towards the pool. At the pool I noticed a thick hemp-braided rope surrounding it. We were given specific instruction that we must either find a place to hold onto the rope, or clear the area and find a place to be seated on the underground deck. We were power walking through a crowd of people to find space at the rope, and after making our way to the farthest wall we were able to find just enough space for the three of us. We were then advised to hold on tight and 'enjoy the ride.'

Slowly, the water began to roll towards us and the sounds of anticipation and excitement matched the waves that were racing our way. We were talking at first, so I didn't really notice the shark swimming towards us in a massive wave. Then, I felt the crash of water against my chest immediately followed by the feeling of wet leather. It was the shark's skin rubbing against me. I remember it feeling calloused and rough, with primal strength and density of the thickest sheet metal. I was in shock. Then, suddenly it hit me: he was targeting me! I knew in an instant that I was in a fight for my life. Wave after wave he seemed to get more precise with his charge. I was reminded of an old movie that I had seen in my younger years as I saw the black eye coming up from the water; I could only pray for a miracle. I looked over for my travel companions and realized that I was alone in this challenge. Literally, everyone that had been playing the 'wave challenge' game had released the rope and I was there all alone. Everyone had moved on.

His eye was like a black pearl and it was trained on me and my destruction. I was fed up with the game and wanted out. I tried to time the wave as perfectly as I could and resolved that with the next wave I would let go and get back to the deck which was apparently safe from shark attacks.

*Wave… crash.... And release!*

I did it!! I was so relieved to be clear of imminent danger that I almost let my guard down completely. That is until I heard Janessa screech, "MOVE, HE IS COMING FOR YOU!!!"

I instinctively dove to my left and just out of the grasp of his jaw, which had broken past the rope barrier for one last ditch effort of pulling me back in with him. I had escaped! My heart was pounding a mile a minute. Never had I known such elation. Fear, anger, joy, resentment, gratitude, all emotions were present. I had just survived the fight of my life.

## Behind the Story

At times we may find ourselves getting so wrapped up in our surroundings that we forget to remain alert to the darkness that exists. Although there is not always the need to have our guard up, we must be aware of our environment and recognize that even the best of intentions can have less than stellar results. Yes, we must give our energy to all things positive. However, we cannot turn a blind eye to murkiness. Truth is, we exist in a world of darkness as well as light, and as mentioned previously, we would be remiss to disavow our reality. The goal is change, but we can't get there by becoming completely oblivious to that which aims to consume us and drag us into their shadows.

Face and address the perceived attacks. By facing our fears, we are able to overcome and discover our true strength.

*Journal Entry: "Attacks"*

There are times when I notice an obvious shift in my energy. It seems as if I struggle to achieve the simplest of tasks, and that I am more inclined to lie down instead of taking care of business. I'm not so totally out of sorts that I get nothing done. Yet, I do recognize that my balance is off. Some call it an off-day. Well, I get *off weeks*. (Without pay)

This is to say that energy is just as crucial as internal light and love. However, I must remain aware that just as with many other things, energy, love and light are frequently sought out by those without it. Generally speaking, the inclination for one to go after that which they desire to possess (regardless of if that thing or item belongs to another) usually leads to attacks. Allow me to clarify.

These attacks can be overt or covert, but the end result is usually some sort of destruction or depletion. Overt attacks are easy to identify. Just think of a common thief and you can easily understand the 'what' and 'how'. Whereas the 'why' is never easily attained unless you have experience in such dealings.

Covert Attacks on the other hand are much more draining. In this particular instance I am referring to the drain on an individual from a spiritual and/or emotional source. This includes but is not limited to the 'me-toos' of the world. A 'me too' being someone that always says that they have experienced the same things as you, no matter the subject. Imagine, if you will, someone that does not allow you to complete a thought before jumping into said notion and capturing it for themselves. Or the person that often enters into conversation with complaints. Or how about the person that you try to help time-and-time-again, but the assistance always seems to blow back in your face; even further, appears to be redirected to you with a mocking undertone? I think you get the picture. Can you sense my frustration?

I really don't like to focus on such negativity. Nevertheless, I am painfully aware that we must understand our struggles in order to truly appreciate and remain in the light of promise. Think of it as an opportunity to free yourself of frustration through understanding and direct communication. I don't feel that many 'me-toos' and energy vampires take action with ill intent. Yet, that does not minimize the results. The bottom line is this: we must remember to protect ourselves at all times. This doesn't mean reconstruct the wall that we've been working so desperately to breakdown. Your heart should remain open and pure, so we must not entertain that which stands to diminish you and your work.

The reality is there will always be a naysayer and those that aim to break down anyone and anything they can. However, recognize that there is no need to remain in the company of those that only offer spiritual depletion if it means becoming some sort of emotional martyr. Instead, just be still and become an active observer. Witness as truth comes to light. Allow the universe to reveal that which should be released and that which should be maintained and nurtured. Although I don't expect this stage to be easy, I do know it's necessary for growth and progress on the path of promise.

Remember, your path will look different from mine. Yet, the ties that bind will remain constant. Is it time for you to look around to evaluate who and what you are allowing into your life and

*This is me today — To stay or go?*

further to identify who is staging the attacks you encounter? Just don't forget to check the mirror as you seek clarity. ♥

## Journal Entry: "Struggles"

We are in a time of monumental struggle; it is a unifying fate that we share from one end of the Earth to another. It is something that no matter our age, sex, creed, financial status, religion, race, etc., we all have as a common thread. Of course this is not our only common thread. However, it is the one that I choose to discuss here.

As for me, I've certainly been no stranger to struggle as a result of my own misappropriation of funds. A little known secret about me: I've had to sleep in my car. I've not known where my next meal would come from. I've had my back so far against the wall that I didn't think I would be able to press forward. However, every time I was met with a hurdle I somehow summoned internal

Begin Your Journey / 73

strength, found my legs and leapt over each obstacle before me. Quite frankly, I AM a survivor.

Again, this isn't about me though. This is about the greater picture. This is about the lessons that come from struggle. So, this is what I know: struggle can sometimes bring a great haze with it. The fog can obscure our vision and cause us to feel anger, grief, resentment, burden, amongst so many other emotions. Yet, once we get through our struggles (individual and collective), we are able to look back with clarity and amazement. It is in these moments of clarity we can count our blessings and see our growth and accomplishments.

Of course when I was in my car trying not to be discovered by those around me in the parking lot, I saw no light. I felt no warmth. All I could do was reflect on how I must've gone wrong in my life. I pondered why karma had chosen to kick me in my moment of loneliness and despair, as I was also going through a very deep depression. It was a very dark and harsh reality. But you know what?! I got through it and I'm much stronger for the experience!

*Hard times serve a purpose*

I know that you are burdened. I know that you have doubts. But trust me when I say HE is forever by your side even as you question HIS presence. And even if you don't believe in HIM, just look to the skies. The universe is much more tangible. Know that when you look up, there are millions of other beings looking up with you. So today don't ignore your struggles or that of your fellow man. Choose instead to relate to your neighbor in the understanding that we never truly know the back story of each other's lives. We don't know what past events caused an individual to build a wall of protection, which only serves to push away those wishing to come close. We don't know why someone chooses to lash out; try your best to respond from understanding instead of assumptions.

What is your struggle? Never be afraid to share that which offers an opportunity to unite. You never know who your truth can help. ♥

~*~*~*~

## What does it all mean?

How are you coming along in your journey? Is anything resonating with you? Can you see glimpses of yourself through my eyes, words and experiences?

Truth is, we are all connected through experiences, feelings and emotions. This is just one of the reasons I put pen to paper so often -- in hopes of highlighting the ties that bind. I choose to stand in the gap for those that may not have their own voice. Yes, we must begin from within, but we must not forget that in the grand scheme of things, we stand united.

## Chapter VII: STANDING IN THE GAP

### NO PASSES

My husband, Chris and I, were home about to begin our day. We were just about to start getting our girls dressed and ready for their dental appointments, but I had to head out to take care of a business matter first. I left to take the bus a single stop from our home because I didn't have the time to walk. Luckily, I caught the bus right away and in less than 5 minutes I was approaching my stop. I stood in front of the rear doors waiting for the light that indicates that it's safe to push the doors open. Yet, the light never came on and the doors never opened for me to exit. The driver started to take off again. I yelled to her that the door didn't open, and when I asked if she could drop me at the nearest corner she refused.

I began to perspire from the anxiety of missing my stop and looked for where the bus was headed next. In my mind, the reality was setting in that my family would never make it to the office appointment in time. I panicked and walked to the front of the bus to plead with the driver to stop, but she kept driving, saying she couldn't let me off until the next designated stop or she would get in trouble with her superiors. The bus kept going and going for what seemed like forever. All I could do was envision how far back I would have to walk with each block that passed.

Once we finally pulled into the bus terminal, I immediately asked for management in order to file a formal complaint. Everyone was then told to remain on the bus so that the management team could conduct an immediate mini-investigation. I explained what transpired and subsequently asked to be compensated for the return cab fare to my original intended destination.

Initially, management disagreed with my terms and said that I would have to cover my own costs. They told me in a rather callous manner that they would take no further action on the complaint as they felt it held no merit. In that moment, I decided to go back to the bus and take an open poll of the passengers that had witnessed the slight. Then, of the people that acknowledged witnessing the obvious error, I asked who was willing to testify on my behalf in open court. There were approximately 10 people that kept their hand raised to my final query. It was only then that the management team agreed to handle my grievance.

They escorted me towards two vehicles. One was a cab and the other a white Crown Victoria. As we were walking, I reminded the gentlemen that I would need at least $20 to cover cab costs. I didn't want to be greedy; I simply wanted justice for the mistake.

At that point, I was asked again if I would consider dropping my complaint. I replied that although I would not pursue further action, I did indeed require transportation and financial compensation to cover the inconvenience. I was then ushered into the back of the white car as I looked towards the cab in confusion. I assumed the cab was to be my method of transportation.

As the gentleman began driving, I had an uneasy feeling come over me. My thoughts began to run rampant.

*"Why wasn't I in the cab?"*

*"Why wasn't the driver speaking to me?"*

*"Why did the other gentlemen take the cab in my place and give me a look of finality?"*

*"Why did I suddenly have two white umbrellas with me?"*

I didn't have much time to ponder my questions when I noticed that we were traveling in the wrong direction. I began to tell the driver the correct directions, but he was unresponsive to my voice. It felt like I wasn't even there. He was so stoic and methodical in his actions. Panic tightened my throat and my stomach began to do flips. Out of instinct, I began to look around the back seat for an escape.

Just then I thought to use the larger umbrella with the metal tip to escape the car by breaking the window after discovering the doors were locked in a manner not allowing me to escape from within. As I attempted my first swing to the back window, the driver began backing the car into a viaduct. He was heading straight into a ditch that was completely filled with water. I immediately realized he had every intention of drowning me!

I swung the umbrella at the window with all my might. Images of my family raced through my mind, giving me strength. I prayed silently and firmly in a way that I had never prayed before. I asked for the strength of God, the angels, the spirits and anyone else that could lend a helping hand. I focused so hard on breaking the window that I didn't even care that my hands bled from the pressure I was putting on the umbrella.

When the driver saw what I was attempting he jumped into the back seat with me. He was too late though. I successfully broke the window and cleared the additional glass with my legs and feet. I struggled with the driver in the back seat for a minute while being pulled into what can only be described as a vacuum or open drain emptying itself of water. I was being sucked down, and all of my attempts to fight only made things worse.

We were both sucked into the drain opening, along with about half of the car, which upon quick observation had the phrase "NO PASSES" marked in bold white letters across the dashboard.

....

I don't know how long I was passed out, but when I came to, I was coughing and disoriented. When I could finally focus I found myself laying next to the same man that had brought me into this situation. Instantly, I was overwhelmed by panic.

*"What if he woke up and decided to finish his job?!"*

I couldn't let him steal me away from my family! I decided to end him before he could end me. I looked around for anything I could use to defend myself and saw the other umbrella. It was still amazingly white even after going through the cesspool of water. It seemed to shine as if being illuminated for my benefit by the heavens.

I grabbed it as quickly as my arms would allow. Then, I clutched it in both hands and held it in the air over my head. I had every intention of hitting this man with it and ending this horrific nightmare once and for all, but just as I went to swing, he woke up!

*"Oh God! Oh God! What should I do?!!!"*

He flipped me as if I was a rag doll and again I found myself with images of my family looping in my head. I could see my husband smiling and playing with our two daughters.

*"What would he tell them if something happened to me? How could he explain that their Mommy was forever gone, and that she would never be able to hug and kiss them again?!"*

*"Lord, I can't let this happen. I need your strength to get me through this. I still have so much more work to do!"*

And with that final prayer; I regained the upper hand in the fight once again. I hit him in the head with everything I could summon, and then some. When I was satisfied that he would not and could not come after me, I dragged myself from the ditch and started for the road. I was so exhausted, yet, somehow found the strength to keep moving forward. I knew from that moment on that I was to do HIS work and biddings. I knew that it was by HIS grace alone that I had survived what should have been my end.

I couldn't wait to get home to my family and hug them all and tell them how much I loved them. From this point on, I vowed to stand up for good, to carry HIS words in my heart, to know and show that we are not alone if we have faith and hold to our prayers. In reality, there was no valid reason as to why I was able to overcome the assassin. He was taller than me, stronger than me and he knew the plan well before anything could register in my mind... This should've been my end, yet it turned into my beginning.

## Behind the Story

Have you ever had a moment in which you found yourself standing in silence although everything in your being screamed for action? Did you walk away from the moment hanging your head and thinking of how you should have reacted differently? Truth is we <u>all</u> have experienced such moments of uncertainty when it comes to standing up for what we feel is righteous. Nevertheless, we mustn't dwell on the inaction. We must focus on the lesson(s) and be determined to grow. It is only in these moments we can truly aim our sights on that which is higher than ourselves.

The errors of my ways are no greater or smaller than anyone else's. However, if we are to grow, we must come to terms with our slights as well as our triumphs. Always give yourself a moment to reflect on the examples of your days. After all, it is always easiest to see the full picture when we stand back to have a better look.

Remember that although standing in the gap for what is righteous may not be easy and may even bring turbulence into our lives. If we stand strong though, with HIM on our side, we can truly overcome anything!

*Yes we can!*

Journal Entry: "Mistake your Kindness"

I don't enjoy confrontation by any means. However, I recognize that I can't be silent in all situations, especially when I'm intrinsically inclined to stand-up for what I believe. I'm going to optimistically assume that is a common thread in most people.

I state that because it is a fact that we are tested on a daily basis. Of course, the extreme to which we are tested as individuals varies greatly. Yet, we are all tested nonetheless. It is in these tests we show our true selves. Lately I've been blessed to recognize my response in the face of tribulations that had the potential to lead me down the road of venomous spite and anger. However, it is through HIS grace that I surprised myself and was able to walk away in a manner that was as dignified as the moment would allow. Please don't mistake me as being cold or removed from the negativity of the overall situation, because I do hurt from the sadness of these types of moments. But I simply choose to move forward. Dwelling simply keeps us stagnant and this is a luxury that I cannot afford.

The thing is, sometimes a muted tongue or censored conversations can be confused for weakness and an inability to stand-up for oneself. When in reality, sometimes self-censorship is necessary to convey a message to someone that might otherwise shield themselves from truly hearing. Think about it. Would you be more prone to listen and learn from someone that approaches you in a calm, yet direct manner? Or someone that charges you with a raised voice?

The bottom-line is regardless of the situation, always be true to whom <u>you</u> are. Don't allow yourself to be reduced by any situation. Yes, at times people will mistake your kindness. But if you are in fact remaining authentic in your intentions and coming from a place of love and light, <u>nothing</u> will be able to break you.

Moving forward, change your perception on what you previously deemed as happening <u>to</u> you. Instead, chuckle and press on past the attempts to prevent your progress. Be thankful for all experiences and recognize the harder someone or something tries to bring you down, the higher you will be able to rise. ♥

*Journal Entry: "Stand Up!"*

I had a moment in which I felt compelled to share my truth with complete transparency and void of censorship. The situation took me completely out of my comfort zone and required that I

*Help @ work*

face slanderous statements that had been strewn about me without regard for the emotional triggers they might unveil. The statements were from an unfortunate event I do not take lightly, even to this day. I will not speak directly to what that issue was because it has been addressed, and I have chosen to move forward. However, for the point of this story I want you to image a cause (any cause) that you hold near to your heart. This event can be good or bad according to your personal perceptions. Now, envision someone *Leanne* unintentionally (or intentionally) making light of that cause or moment with others simply to provoke a reaction from you.

Would you say something? Would you address the elephant in the room, or would you choose to walk by as if there was nothing obstructing your views or path?

Well, I feel as though I've met a few occasions that lent an opportunity for me to stand up for what I felt was right and 'good'. I'm not hailing myself as a saint or even a trailblazer, but I do feel that these moments serve as tests. These occurrences test us as individuals and as collective souls by eliciting organic responses that cannot be pre-scripted.

Yes, I must admit that I've been highly sensitive to such matters; which I now understand is because I am a sensitive intuitive that picks up on the emotions of others whether those emotions are latent or blatant. Yet, I do believe in taking up the proverbial flag for those that are hurt in silence.

Let me reiterate that I am not attempting to take on the role of hero. I'm just stating what must be said. Today and moving forward, I will no longer find satisfaction in silence and 'knowing my role' when faced with potential negativity. Instead I will stand-up in love and light to represent that which aims to resolve conflict through loving coexistence! Now my question for you is, will you do the same? ♥

*Journal Entry: "Guard your Words"*

I used to think that saying whatever was on my mind -- regardless of content -- was just me 'keeping it real'. I figured that if the person on the receiving end didn't want to hear what I had to say, they could leave my presence. Thinking of it now makes me realize how far I would go in being ruthless with the depth of my insensitivities.

Don't get me wrong, I do believe that we all have the right to be assertive and stand up for ourselves under the right circumstances. However, I don't think that cruelty has to be included in the delivery. Sometimes holding back is necessary. It does not make you fake. Quite the contrary, it makes you human.

Therefore, moving forward, we must be cautious and guard our words; not to the point of minimizing our issues, but within reason. It's as simple as asking yourself the following questions before speaking:

- ☐ Is it true?
- ☐ Is it necessary?
- ☐ Is it kind?

Based on your responses, you will know if you should move forward with your words. Just remember that conversations, although they may seem harmless and/or superficial, have a tendency to stay with people. Understand that just as you share your truth through compassion, the person on the receiving end is free to respond as they deem fit. However, by guarding your words, you are taking steps to emit that which you wish to receive. ==Stand firm in your truth, but remember to carry love and light in your heart as you shine your light upon others.== Those that are willing and ready will understand, whilst others are not obligated to share your views. ♥

~*~*~*~

### What does it all mean?

Now that you've read about a few of my moments, are you able to reflect on your opportunities to stand in the gap for yourself or another? Did you mind your words in effort to ensure you were not aiming to harm? Trust me, I understand that these steps along the path to positive change are not simple by any means. We are all constant works in progress. However, this isn't about perfection - outside of striving to consistently become a perfect version of yourself within each moment that is presented to you. This is about remaining as diligent and steadfast as you can because there will be challenges, and it is important to stay focused in those times when darkness attempts to derail your success.

## Chapter VIII: OVERCOMING THE ENEMY AGAINST ALL ODDS

### DANGEROUS CREATURES

I used to live in a white castle. Well, it wasn't really a castle, but it was my family and my little piece of the world, and we were happy with it. True, it might not have held the material means of those of a higher financial standing, but I never seemed to notice. Of course, like any household, we had our issues. However, I could never have imagined the dangers that would soon befall my family and me.

It seemed as if the house had grown in size since my last visit, which was strange because usually childhood homes seem smaller upon return. Nevertheless, I knew it was the same place where I was raised. We were packing boxes to get ready to move after being informed the land was now unsafe for human inhabitance. Strange thing was that the area had suddenly been taken over by creatures. What used to be a suburban home in an urban neighborhood was now in the midst of what grew to resemble a dangerous rain forest. There were snakes every few steps, even coming up from the ground beneath the trees which had sprouted to heights far above anything I had ever seen. They blocked views in all directions and prevented anyone from seeing upcoming hazards. It was as if everything had changed literally over night and we were suddenly being forced to evacuate! I couldn't believe my eyes. How could this be real?

After a long day of packing, it was evident everyone was tired. Yet, we could not afford to stop for the day because each moment that passed brought with it more of the perils that lurked beyond the manmade walls. Instead, I decided to prepare a late lunch in order to provide a much needed energy boost and return some pep to our packing. As I headed into the kitchen, I noticed that the back door had been left ajar. Under normal circumstances this would not serve as a problem. However, what used to be a backyard now resembled a very deadly jungle. The grass had grown at record speeds and was cloaking its venomous inhabitants who were bent on overtaking anything or anyone that threatened its turf.

I was infuriated by this oversight. How could someone be so careless? I made my frustrations known, verbally, as I hurried to close the door. Yet, it was too late. Animals, mostly serpents, had already made their way pass the door. I quickly shut the door and with what could only be described as some sort of animalistic instinct, I started to grab them with my bare hands one-by-one and started ripping their heads off. I kept thinking about my babies being inside, and there was nothing that I would not do to ensure their safety. Any hesitation on my part in this situation could prove fatal to the ones that I cared for most.

It's funny when you contemplate the way "fight-or-flight" works. Had it been any other day or any other circumstances, I would have been repulsed at the mere thought of touching what I considered to be such a vile creature. However, in this moment, I could not grab them fast enough. There was no time to spare. My role as guardian and protector was in full gear, not just for my children, but for the sake of everyone in the house.

As quickly as I could move, I ended each one. Rip - rip – rip! Their heads were separated clean from their bodies. I tossed the carcasses down in the same swift moment as I would pick up the next one. I was almost expecting them to slither away to try and save their own lives as they saw me coming. Instead, these cold blooded creatures forged ahead without any regard for their fellow brothers and sisters. They were now seeking refuge in what used to be the safe haven of my youth, and they sought sustenance in aiming to strike at my very own children and kin.

Mid-thought, I noticed that a small, very deadly serpent managed to make its way into the house and had its sights set for my child. I screamed, warning everyone to be on high alert, and then I grabbed a meat cleaver to go after the beast. My movements were just as trained as that of the snake, more so. My attention was focused. I aimed to end this dangerous creature before it could even get near my baby. Then, suddenly, I noticed I had been bitten. There was no time for hesitation. "I am a machine," I said to myself, "a machine that runs on adrenaline alone and I don't feel a thing."

Unknown to my oldest child, the animal continued to make its way towards her. The innocence of her childhood prevented her from sensing the imminent danger. I yelled for her to move in the exact minute that it attempted to strike. As it moved in, so did I summoning all the fury and energy I could muster. The meat cleaver was an extension of me, and in one fail swoop, I sliced the would-be murderer in half. Amazingly enough, my daughter somehow remained oblivious to the entire incident. "Thank God," I thought. My home was safe again from the danger of evil's intrusion. I breathed a sigh of relief and held my babies closer than ever before, not wanting to let go.

As for the bite, well, I became woozy once the shock began to wear off. Then I could hear the whispers around me as I began to black out. They said, "Marisa, you are not done yet. You have greater work to do." With that, I awoke to a throbbing bruise. Though excruciating, it was the beginning of my miraculous recovery. I now know that HE saved me once again. No weapons formed against me shall prosper. Not mental, physical or emotional!

*That right!!*

## Behind the Story

Dangerous creatures can come in many different forms. Make sure that YOU are ready to be a soldier for good when facing evil. Of course the physical attack is a representation of the 'evil' that lurks around our daily existence. Yet, even this notion is up to interpretation. However, real danger does exist in this world and its reality can often make the journey to change quite turbulent. It is the things in life that serve to make us weary, which are the very reasons our journey is necessary.

Do you ever find yourself feeling small in comparison to the tasks ahead of you? Well, this is all a part of the process of change, and you are certainly not alone. When we begin from within and take responsibility for ourselves that is the moment we can, and do affect, change.

*Journal Entry: "Weary but Hopeful"*

Not so long ago, my days started very early, being awake in mind before the sun even kissed the sky. I was inclined to update social media sites before drifting back to sleep as quickly and easily as I had awoken. I guess you could say something or someone else was willing me to do those things, because once I was completely awake (*2-hours later*), I found myself reviewing my updates and posts as if I were looking at the work of a stranger. This happened often. However, on this particular day, these actions made an existential impact on the day ahead.

My mantra for the day was, "Today, I will think before I speak and not allow the enemy to control my actions."

Why didn't I take heed of my own words?! As soon as I had

officially woken-up, it was as if the enemy had aligned my actions to lead my heart into such a dark spiral of uncertainty and hurt, before I could take pause to evaluate the situation. I had already taken action on two people that have been known to resuscitate me in my darkest hours. It was through them that I found a strong part of my voice and became comfortable with my quirky ways. They had done nothing that would illicit my overreaction under normal circumstances, but again... I hadn't taken pause to discern what was happening in the moments that I perceived as betrayal. Instead of doing so and guarding my words, I dove in with anger, resentment and untruths.

Here is what I know. The enemy uses haste to carry out his agenda. I'm not suggesting that we dwell on things with the exception of meditation, where we dwell on clarity in and of itself. I'm suggesting that we must THINK before taking action. This won't stop us from making false steps, but it will lessen its likelihood.

This journey has been strenuous, daunting, joyous, enlightening, burdensome, confusing, exhilarating and most other words you can think of to express emotions. I often find myself struggling on a regular basis to not break under the weight of overcoming inclinations to overreact. Alas, I find reassurance in knowing that there are no real mistakes on the path of life, just detours and, the knowing we would not have been chosen to walk this path if we were not capable of seeing things through. However, we are only human, we make mistakes, we experience emotional swings, and we all get weary.

Yes, we might be weary, but we must hold firm to hope by resting assured in knowing that the tough times shall pass, we just have to be willing to face those moments directly and continue to forge ahead. ♥

*Journal Entry: "Answers"*

I had a moment. It could have been bad, but I chose to make it good. I took that moment to reflect and pray for a response that was not from my ego, but from HIM. I asked that I be shown the truth in what I was feeling, and no sooner did the prayers leave my mind that the answers appeared. No, it wasn't an obvious response, but it was a response nonetheless. I am grateful that I don't have to carry the burden of concern by looking for answers amidst darkness.

Life can be beautiful if you allow it to be. Yes, negativity tries to interfere with peace. I still have waves of anxiety and emotion. Yet, the beauty in my response to the enemy at these times of looming self-doubt and turmoil is to grant him no more than a chuckle. I chuckle because I know the enemy is a liar and I know that he is desperately searching the darkness to grab a hold of me to keep me where he feels I should be. However, at this point I have already been shown the way to the light and have no reason to look back.

So, when there is a moment of question or doubt, simply turn your sights towards the light. In it, you too can find the answers you seek. You simply need to be still and willing to see them and accept them regardless of your expectations. ♥

*Journal Entry: "Growth"*

    I took an online course some time ago. This typically wouldn't be an event that would illicit mention, except I really participated. Again, this may not seem like a big deal, except I <u>never</u> participate in classes or situations that require interaction. I mean never. Usually, I am the person that tries to blend in with my surroundings for fear of being noticed. I can have a million questions on the tip of my tongue but I choke on the words before they can leave my mouth. Yet still, for this course I came prepared. I had tons of questions locked and loaded. I shared personal experiences and things that I typically have only shared with less than a handful of people.

    What's the big deal you ask? Everything. In that moment, I embraced the opportunity presented and accepted the growth that it provided. I made the conscious decision to not allow my fear and insecurities to prevent me from taking another step closer to my destiny.

    The bottom line is that we cannot allow anyone or anything to stifle our ability to grow and progress in what we know is meant for us. When we are happy and confident in our destinies, the enemy is aggravated; so aggravate away! HIS plan for us is perfect. We only need to embrace it and release the fear associated with the unknown. ♥

*Journal Entry: "Calling the Enemy's Bluff"*

It was a beautiful morning. I woke up on the right side of bed and felt ready to conquer the world, even without my morning cup of coffee. The sun was shining bright, birds were singing, my kids were eating their breakfast without complaints, and I could feel positive energy all around. Then, noon hit.

All of a sudden, it was as if the world had turned on its head and all that was right, was now wrong. A feeling of despair washed completely over me and sunk deep within my core. I didn't understand it, let alone know how to rid myself of it.

Thoughts of old hurts came into my mind. My children were completely wired and I felt overwhelmed and depressed. Then, I prayed.... I prayed for guidance. I prayed for help. I prayed for mercy. HIS response led me to address the hurt in order to get it off my chest. I did, and praise HIS name, I found resolution. I simply had to speak up for myself and make my needs known. Then things lined up so that I could get the much needed reprieve I didn't even realize I desperately needed. HE took my burdens away. *Puerto Rico*

I am so grateful and blessed by HIS glory. Today, I called the enemy's bluff by not allowing myself to be swept into the pit of despair. I claim dominion over my feelings and needs, in turn finding the peace I desperately sought. I could've wallowed in my misery and shutdown to any attempts of overcoming the darkness into which I found myself falling. In this time of desperation though, I chose to become the hero of my story. I took action to turn things around. Yes, you might find me down in tough moments of sorrow, but trust and believe that I will never be out.

♥

~*~*~*~

### What does it all mean?

Truth be told, things will come up that challenge your new direction. It can be something as simple as a good friend mocking your new way of being or telling you how much you've changed. Which, if you think about it is quite ironic, seeing as how that is the entire point of this journey. So why, in turn, would you become offended when someone suggests that you have changed? I will use this point to illustrate how our perceptions in fact shape our realities.

We can only be offended by that which we allow to offend. We have choices along this path, and those choices lend to real outcomes. This is why it is so important to claim your power, by calling dominion over your free-will and deciding consciously to use it towards reflecting that which you wish to receive. Which direction and which choices will you decide to make? Will you stay the course, or will you turn off track?

## Chapter IX: THE RELEASE

### OVER THE EDGE

I had a vision that I was driving a jeep on a leisure trip to clear my head. It was a bright and sunny day outside and the scenery made me think of LA: palm trees, sun, beach, and the like. (All the things you would imagine.)

As I was cruising along, I started feeling freer and more secure with each mile. Therefore, I accelerated a bit. The thing is, I was new to the area and didn't know the lay of the land. But, I was feeling fancy-free at this point as I was practically flying down the road without a care in the world. At least until I approached the tracks.

I saw the gate coming down but was going too fast to stop, so I had to make the decision. Go even faster to try and get through or to try and stop. I chose to punch it. Except, there were more than one set of tracks, so I needed to figure out which set the train was coming on to avoid uncertain doom. I thought I had figured it out when I looked up and noticed all tracks ran parallel to a cliff. I was so focused on figuring out the right track that I didn't notice I was running out of road.

It was too late to reverse, too late to change things. I could only go forward into certain descent. I closed my eyes, sought peace, and prayed to and for my loved ones. I accepted my fate and surrendered to HIM. Everything went silent; everything was so still and peaceful. I felt weightless.

When I crashed over the cliff, I was conscious. My eyes opened slowly to my surroundings; I was engulfed in a cloud. Was I alive?

## Behind the Story

We all experience moments that are both within our control and outside of our control. The key in both scenarios is to maintain serenity in order to be able to differentiate one from the other. Are you in a moment that requires you to take the reigns and lead the charge? Or does your current situation call for you to let go and accept things as they occur? Ultimately, free-will allows us to choose the path we take on this journey. However, it is your decisions that determine the steps that will create the path.

*Yes*

Journal Entry: "Let it go"

I have found that I have the habit of holding on to things that aren't necessarily in HIS plan for me. We hold on tight because it's either familiar or, on the polar opposite end, because it's such a break from the norm that it gives us a rush of excitement.

In reality, we must learn how to let go when the time is right. We must pay attention to the signs that tell us things or people aren't right for us. We must openly acknowledge our correct paths, and in-turn, remove anything that is either derailing or destroying our progress.

Ask yourself:

- ☐ Does this make me a better person?
- ☐ Does this get me closer to my goals?
- ☐ Does this feel like my true future?
- ☐ Does this feel equal?

If the answers are negative, then you probably know what you should do already. Sometimes the steps on our paths aren't easy, but they are always necessary. Think of it this way: if you hold on to something or someone that is not a part of your destiny, you are also removing that person from their righteous path. The choice is yours, so this is where you must consider. Where should you go from here? ♥

*Journal Entry: "Releasing Labels"*

There has always been some unspoken restraint placed on me. Don't be too loud, stop being so crazy, fit in, squeeze into the mold that society creates, and focus on what *we* tell you. The list is endless. I was always smashed into a box labeled in accordance with "society's standards" and I lost all feeling and touch with the true me. A lifetime seems just long enough to remove all identity from a person.

Shrinking was a product of my low self-esteem. Make jokes at my own expense, belittle my accomplishments, and lower my voice when speaking of my leaps, while shouting the strides of another from the tallest mountaintops. I was creating a world of solitude that holds the keys to my very essence; only allowing others to have the slightest glimpse into my world for fear of judgment, when in reality, it was I that was doling out the judgments against me.

Fact of the matter is, I am my harshest critic. I often prevent myself from blossoming into the person I am meant to be for fear of how others will perceive me. I've always kept a side of myself locked away so tightly because I didn't want to be labeled as a weirdo. But in reality, who cares what others think?! Of course I mean that in the most loving way possible. Yes, I am a multitude of things: forever growing, forever learning and forever changing. I'm still tempted to offer labels as a means of comfort for myself and others, but I am learning to just be me.

In each passing second since my decision to reclaim my existence and embark on this journey of change, I am rediscovering the beauty that lies within my soul. I used to think that modesty as it related to who I am and what I do, or anything that pertained to me, was crucial in order to have friends and/or fit into the bigger picture. However, what I failed to realize is that others are not able to grow any taller by my shrinking into the shadows. In doing so, I'm only offering a false sense of accomplishment to those around me. Instead, in order to grow, we must all let go of our self-inflicted restraints and coexist within our individual truths. This includes me being able to stand tall and fully display my spirit to encourage others to do the same.

*Speak up / Be willing to let go / Staying Quiet*

It's time to let everything else go. I am not my past. I am not my future. I just am. ♥

*Journal Entry: "Let it go II"*

I noticed that one of my most popular blog posts to date was "Let it go". The reason I mention this is because apparently this is a struggle that most people can relate to, present company included. Why do we hold on so tightly to things that are not for us? Whether that be a friendship, romantic tie, acquaintance, or even a pair of pants that no longer fit. (Just making sure you're still paying attention.)

We need to truly evaluate where we are versus where we need or want to be when looking at these relationships. If you feel that you deserve better, prove it by turning your words into action. It's easy to complain about what is wrong in our lives, but it takes courage to actually stand in the gap and affect change.

Take control of your life. Wish those that don't belong as main characters in the play of your life well, and then move on! The past exists to provide lessons and stories, not to find a cozy spot to camp out and in-turn prevent productivity and happiness. After all, if you aren't moving forward, then you are standing still or worse moving backwards.

Remember, a vehicle without an engine is typically just scrap. Let go and move forward. ♥

~*~*~*~

What does it all mean?

One of the most difficult parts of my journey has been letting go of my controlling ways. Did I mention I have the tendency to be a control freak? I have to fight the knee-jerk reaction to monitor and hover over all things. Truth is, I'm not in control of most things; instead it is simply an illusion that I have created for myself as a means of comfort. Where the reality shows that the universe, the source, God, the higher power (wherever you place your faith), is truly the one in control. Everything we need to be happy, to coexist and to love is innately within our being. The trick is in releasing what we have been programmed to do in order to remember our truths, and this, my soul friends, requires us to often step outside of our comfort zones.

## Chapter X: STEP OUTSIDE OF YOUR COMFORT ZONE

### VISIONS

I had a vision of myself at a pool party with tons of people. I was playing hostess although it wasn't my event, I was making sure everyone had what they needed, fulfilling my unspoken purpose of bringing order to what I would have considered an otherwise chaotic scene. There were two activities going on at once and things were quite hectic, but it appeared as if everyone was having a great time nonetheless. There was the main pool party taking place outside and simultaneous card games occurring inside. There were no places for boredom to manifest.

As I was cleaning and wrapping stuff up indoors, I noticed things were getting unruly outside. All I could hear was yelling and the sound of people crowding around in one space. By the time I made my way to the scene, I saw that Tera and Theresa -- sisters that attended high school with me -- were attempting to drown someone. I ran over as quickly as I could to immediately put a stop to such violent acts. My heart was pounding in my ears; I couldn't believe what was taking place. Had I missed something? Then I realized what was happening. They were blaming the death of another on their victim. In that moment, I told them that one life for another was not worth it, and it would only perpetuate the cycle of violence that so desperately needed to end. I told them they have much better things to focus on such as family, friends and love, and they shouldn't throw everything away on revenge and blind rage.

After they stopped the attack, two other girls approached me. They were escorting an elderly woman who seemed to have trouble seeing and speaking. She grabbed on to me so tightly I couldn't move, even when I tried to pull away with all my might.

She started saying things into my ear that I couldn't understand. I was somewhat afraid, but mostly intrigued. I felt what she was saying would help me on my path and that she knew things about my gifts that no one else dared to confess publicly.

Moments later, the woman was gone and I was in a new house completely removed from the festivities that had taken place moments earlier. It was as if I were transported to another place and time altogether, but still with the girls that had originally escorted me away from the chaos. I felt uncomfortable with the unfamiliar surroundings, but strangely enough there was a familiar feeling as well. It was as if I were in a dream; one that I had already had in a previous life or perhaps it was something that I had experienced in my waking life but suppressed.

One of the girls asked me if I remembered what happened, referring to my conversation with the elderly woman. I told her that I did, but that I didn't know what the woman had said to me because I couldn't understand her. I felt frustrated and kept trying to repeat her words in my mind over-and-over because my soul could sense the significance of every syllable she spoke to me. She was telling me all that I ever wished to know, all that I had ever questioned within myself. She had the key to my very existence and I couldn't recall her words. The girl then instructed someone else to play a record. I was so lost in my own sadness though; that I didn't recognize initially the very thing I was trying so desperately to recall was being played openly for my private audience.

I was astonished at what I was hearing. The woman that spoke into my ear during the tight embrace said that I was meant to do great things. She said that I have many visions, but would begin having many, many more. She told me that I would hear things and people in ways I never thought possible.

I started sobbing uncontrollably. Not out of fear, but out of relief, acceptance and anticipation. I finally felt validation for everything I had been experiencing throughout my entire life. I wasn't crazy! I felt that my greater purpose was finally being revealed. I recognized that I was walking the path God had set for me. I was completely overwhelmed with emotion, and I didn't try to fight it. My shoulders gave way to the burden and doubt I had been carrying my entire life. I was finally free to become who I was always meant to be.

In that moment, I asked to speak with the woman again, to thank her for helping me, for being the vessel of my understanding. It was then the oldest girl brought me a book with a piece of paper marking a specific page. She didn't speak, she just handed me the book. I was confused but went ahead and followed her unspoken directions and opened the book. It was a bible, and in it I was stunned to see the funeral program and obituary for the woman I had spoken to. She had been deceased for 10 years.

## Behind the Story

Some things in life simply cannot be explained. They are supernatural experiences that either strengthen or crush our faith. We must accept that life is not about always having a neat definition for what we see and experience. More often than not, we simply need to act in faith and acceptance because there is reality beyond what the human eye can behold. Are you ready and willing to step outside the box of comfort and conformity, and admit that you know there is more to our existence than what typical society wants you to acknowledge?

*Journal Entry: "I can only be me"*

Can I say something quickly? I really love the person I'm becoming. No, I don't mean to sound arrogant, it actually still takes a lot for me to even *say* that aloud. You see, I have been trying to focus on my self-confidence a bit more lately. For instance, sometimes when I do a reading and the recipient turns away a statement that I give, I feel as if I want to just shut that side of me off completely. I get emotions of utter embarrassment and feel like a complete failure and fraud. I start thinking about all the articles and conversations mentioning fake psychics and connect myself to them immediately. What can I say; I can be pretty drastic in my responses. It's a part of my extreme sensitivity.

Begin Your Journey / 121

Yet, it never fails that HE stays true to boosting my confidence by proving my visions correct. Sometimes it happens right away, and other times it takes a while for the proverbial a-ha moment to strike. For instance, I may tell someone that a butterfly has appeared to them, offering a sign of transformation. Yet, the person rejects the notion saying that they haven't seen a butterfly and they don't even like the insect. Moments later, someone else speaks to the same person and mentions a moth and it is confirmed with great vigor. I'm left reading along and wondering, "WTF?" to myself, a moth/butterfly; you got the drift. To take things further, the person agrees that they have just experienced a major shift in recent days and have come out like a new person. WHAT?! It can still be quite frustrating.

I originally thought it was my ego getting in the way by distorting my perception of the feedback I was receiving. However, in reality, I just didn't trust myself and was hesitant in believing my own visions; which in turn was transferring to the recipient. When I trust in myself and believe in what is given to me --whether it is a message, vision, dream, empathic emotion, etc.,-- I recognize that I must truly operate on faith in order to push beyond the potential for a dark hold over my mindset. I receive that which I emit. Get it?!

All of this to say that I am finally coming into my own and although I've never been one to toot my own horn, in this moment I realize that I am so much more than I've given myself credit for. I am beginning to see through my own veil of lies, I know things that many may never experience, and I embrace the fact that there is more than meets the eye. But I can't convince anyone of my knowledge, especially if I don't wholly trust and believe it myself. Now is the time to embrace myself and trust that as long as my heart is in the right place, and I do no harm to others, things will fall into place. ♥

*Journal Entry: "A Lucid Dream"*

What if I were to tell you that the world you see in front of you is simply an elaborate illusion? What if I said you need only look to the sky to see the evidence of us all existing within the brush strokes of a great creator? Would you believe me or would you dismiss my words no sooner than they registered in your mind?

Each moment, each step, each word has been carefully drawn with love and purpose in the nanosecond prior to the moment occurring. Yes, we all have the free-will to choose which direction we turn, but the creator of whom I speak, has the scripted version of our actions long before the script can even be written. The world is painted on so many different planes, that all of our potential decisions and actions have already been mapped accordingly.

I offer this grand hypothetical to not only give you reason to take pause during your reading to look towards the skies, but to create a spark of curiosity in pondering the possibilities that exist. As beings of the Earth, we covet the ability to label and define all that we see, hear, smell, touch and taste. But what about that sixth sense? We find comfort in the tangible or side-eye and scoff at that which we cannot explain or fully comprehend.

If I were to tell you that this life is simply a lucid dream or out of body experience that served to test our souls in consideration of the next phase to which we will travel after these Earthly lives are done, would you re-evaluate you life decisions? Would you take care and use compassion when deciding to judge the life and actions of another? Would you stop in your tracks to evaluate your decisions that you've made up until this point?

The point is we choose to accept that which can be proven because most other things beyond the scope of understanding and comfort lead to uncertainty. Uncertainty then leads to discomfort, which in turn leads to dismissal, because if I can't understand it, I cannot embrace it. Is this truly how you want to exist? I propose that we consciously choose to be present within the endless possibilities that reside outside and within ourselves. Let us dwell in the notion that we are living in a dream, and as we all know, dreams are temporary. Let's live this dream by claiming our individual and collective power towards becoming the change we wish to see in this world, because sooner or later, we are bound to wake-up. ♥

## Journal Entry: "My Truths"

I had a dream that five eagles flew down from the heavens and landed right at my feet. They were larger than any animal I had ever encountered, and they were standing tall directly in front of me. Yet, I felt no fear. I was initially startled by the swiftness with which they arrived until I had the realization that they were being presented as gifts from above. Then, one-by-one, each of them transformed in tangible items; the one that stood out to me the most was the nesting dolls. I reached my hand forward to grab them and a large, ravenous wolf appeared. Although I knew he was a wolf of ill intent, he was manifest in human form; and though I could see his true nature, to everyone else he was a mere man.

His voice was booming and harsh, and I could see in his spirit that he wanted nothing good for me. He wanted to covet me in the same manner that a young boy would covet a new video game system. I was nothing more than property and a pretty face. He took me from my home, promised to take care of me, and then abandoned me in the slums. He somehow managed to remove my memory of the eagles that had been presented to me. It was as if I was made a pawn in a silent game the rules of which I was not privy. I felt in my heart that I was meant for something greater than myself, but didn't know how to obtain it. First I needed to find my way out of the gutter in which this wolf in sheep's clothing had stranded me. I was solely operating on the imprinted instructions that the almighty had sewn into the fiber of my being. I made so many wrong decisions in the process of my return to grace, it was like I was searching for a light switch in the midst of the deepest catacombs.

My angels must've been guiding me along the way because, although I had no true intentions of turning my life around, and my spirit had given up, I always found myself pushing for more. Yet, towards the end of my journey towards the light, it was as if my steps had become second nature. It was amazingly reassuring. I was making my way back to the light from which I had originally come.

~*~*~*~

What does it all mean?

Oftentimes our dreams serve as visual manifestations of our past, present and future realities. My journey has brought me to a much higher spiritual plane and is truly revealing my truths and those of so many around me. Just as shown in my aforementioned dream, I have made a great many mistakes in my life. However, as I sit here going over past moments in my mind, I find myself hard pressed to even continue to label my past as a mistake because every decision I've made and every step I've taken has led me to this very moment. Sure, I might have made my journey a bit longer and even rougher, but in the grand scheme of things, we cannot look back with regret. Instead, we should embrace everything for the lessons learned and the wisdom gained.

This is our opportunity to use the stepping stones of yesterday to rebuild our paths and continue moving forward with an even deeper understanding and strength.

Chapter XI: REBUILDING AND MOVING FORWARD

UNDER CONSTRUCTION

I had a vision that my friends, family and I were in a social hall that was set-up inside of a gymnasium. We were talking about random things and making general conversation. Then, as I looked out of the window, I noticed that the clouds were making various conspicuous shapes. I pointed it out to everyone. At first no one saw what I was referring to, and then slowly it was as if the clouds began to shift like they were being meticulously sculpted into various works of art to illustrate my words. Every detail was formed into the clouds as if they were made of clay. I began to get lost in the shapes, so much so, that I barely noticed when he left the table, especially since he was sitting at the opposite end from me. Once I checked back into reality after being lost in the clouds, I saw that he had taken the children as he left. I didn't panic because there was an event going on in the various rooms of the building we were in, so I figured he had taken them to one of them for a different activity being that they get bored from sitting still too long. After all, they are children.

As I searched for him, I could feel the panic set in. Every hallway seemed to stretch on forever and every corner seemed to have a hidden corridor that I needed to explore in hopes of discovering their whereabouts. With each passing second that we were apart, I began to grow weary. Every question I had posed to those that crossed my path was greeted with a shrug of uncertainty.

Then finally, I forced a classroom door open and heard my youngest child's voice. She was in a playpen nearest the door in a room of strangely disheveled men. I walked in without hesitation and grabbed her out of the playpen while my eyes scoured the room for him and our other two children. I initially spotted him attempting to blend into the room by shrinking into his chair for fear that I would cause a scene. Then, I saw my other babies. I instructed my children to come from the corner where they were playing and told them to come with me; we were leaving. They seemed more than happy to oblige. Before exiting, I started talking to him and asked why he would leave without letting me know his destination. Initially he was quiet, and then he admitted that it was because he was angry at me for controlling the conversation and attention in the main hall from which we originally came. He said that it was not my personality. Rather, he was the one that always controls the room in social situations. His actions indicated a desire for me to leave permanently.

Just then, someone else in the room decided to chime in on our conversation. The gentleman spoke to me in a callous manner, and was basically telling me I should know my role as wife and mother; I must let the man lead everything. I advised this man to mind his own personal dealings and to stay out of things he could never comprehend.

I walked out of the classroom with our children in tow, with him following closely behind. His head hung low, but I couldn't tell if it was from defeat or shame.

As I turned down another corridor, I realized that once again I was walking alone with only a baby in my arms. The baby was wrapped in a large blue blanket, but my mind thought in pronouns of "she". Eventually, my baby and I made our way to a hallway that was under construction. There was only one female worker on duty, but she was off in the far end of the hall in a glass enclosed room that resembled a parking garage cashier booth. The strange thing was there was a family living in this corridor. A grandmother and her two grandchildren; a blonde- haired, brown- eyed boy, and girl, both of which were about 5 and 9 years of age respectively. They were living within the confines of the construction zone. The grandmother cooked on a hot plate as the children ran back and forth through the hall. Once again, I found myself strangely intrigued by them and my attention was pulled from my original thoughts to the homeless family before me. As I walked closer, I noticed the floor wasn't complete. It had gaps that were camouflaged with red carpet runners like that of an award show entrance. The floor consisted of two-story construction pillars which stood above a sidewalk, concrete bed. I froze. I realized that if these children continued at play, something bad was....

Too late! The boy fell through the floor gaps but was holding onto a metal barb for dear life. I encouraged him to keep holding on so I could get help. I got the attention of the construction worker and she, having not noticed the family before, was initially startled that so many people were in the construction area. She knew she didn't have time to reprimand anyone because she had to save the boy. The construction worker got out her tools and started building the room around him.

I kept wondering why she didn't call for help or use a ladder to reach him. And just then, almost as if she read my thoughts, she stated, "There is no one to call, everyone is already gone and this boy doesn't have time to wait on 2nd shift".

Without warning, I felt the runner give way under my feet. I couldn't grab for anything because I was holding my baby. Then, in what felt to be extreme slow motion we began to fall deeper and deeper into the space between the pillars with only the carpeting supporting our weight. Suddenly though, the fall was stopped by something. I didn't know what it was, but felt thankful for it. I went to check on my baby and was met with a harsh reality: there was no baby! I had been holding an empty blanket the entire time. My mind was racing, "Did someone take the baby without me knowing? How did I not realize that there was no baby in my arms?!"

Just then, I looked up from my internal conversation in time to notice that the boy is not only free, but running around again. "Really?!" I thought to myself, "Kids, they never learn!" Then I noticed something, I thought to myself, "Wait, what is he holding? That's my wallet!" I yelled, "Hey kid, give me my wallet! Once I get out of here, I'm going to get you!" My words fell upon deaf ears as I thought, "Why isn't he listening to me?" Then, he started to read my information out loud.

> *"Marisa I-I-ik-poh. According to her social media page, she has two kids and one on the way... She's due in two weeks"*

"Wait, what?!" I said internally.

I started crying uncontrollably but no one paid me any attention.

*"This must be why there is no baby: When did I die?"*

## Behind the Story

Oftentimes, we lose track of what is truly occurring within the moments of our lives. We are living in the past or focused on the future so diligently that we tend to forget about the present moment. This is where the notion of grounding comes into play. Grounding is simply the ability to recognize and truly live within the current moment as it is taking place. It is not about daydreaming or having the "woulda-coulda-shoulda's". It is simply about breathing and accepting the brilliance that lies within the here and now.

*Journal Entry: "Get Grounded"*

Every now and again, I find myself getting carried away within my own thoughts. I tend to imagine catastrophe and to even mind-read, or peer into the future when I don't know what is around the corner in my life. It's my controlling side rearing its ugly head again. This is why I'm so thankful for the grounding elements in my life; my family. Simply put, they help me in my struggles.

I find this is why grounding is such an important part of my life within this journey, especially in those moments I have the propensity to allow things and people to divert me from my path. In these moments, I find myself being pulled into the storms of others, or feeding into the notions of inadequacy. Truth is, I can't allow myself to be pulled down those paths, and neither can you because in doing so, we simply create our own detours on the road to our destiny. Instead, we must ground ourselves in the here and now and grant ourselves moments of clarity to make the best possible decision regarding our next steps towards change. ♥

Help God

*Journal Entry: "Sync your Steps"*

I often look at messages on social media at the worst times. I can be running around like mad and take a quick glance at the tablet or laptop just to see that telling, blinking message box, or that number indicator showing that a message awaits. I tell myself I have entirely too much going on to stop in my tracks and check the message, but that darned curiosity always gets the best of me. I mean, what if someone needs me?! What if there is a free grocery giveaway around the corner from me that will end within the next 30-minutes?! What if I have to spring into action to save the world?!

Okay, I'm well aware that these what-ifs are highly unlikely. However, I mention them to express how my mind works. These are my <u>real</u> thoughts, people. I don't go small on anything, or if I do go small, it's only a stepping stone to the progressive thoughts that fill my head at any given moment. I mention this for a couple of different reasons.

- Why in the world do I always look at these messages, knowing full and well the time it takes to read them is time taken from my chaotic tasks of the moment?

- When I read these messages, of course I am most likely running short on time and have no business taking even a second to respond. Yet, I always do. Or at least I do in my mind. Seriously, I think out a full response that is often in such detail that later when it's time to make the actionable response, I think I already have! *Tell me I'm not alone in this.*

This means I've got way too much going on at once and I am spreading myself too thin. Oftentimes, I find my mind gets out of sync with my actions, especially when I forget to ground myself, meditate or simply seek balance. It's the mental equivalent to having a to-do list that entails picking up five items from five different stores, and then choosing to pick-up one item from each store in shifts until I have all 25 items. It just doesn't make sense! Why would we choose to work harder instead of smarter?

When things get overwhelming and thoughts don't seem to sync with actions, I now recognize this is a true-fire sign I need to slow down and take a step back from the chaos to just breathe. I must then review the situation to determine its importance and remind myself that although I am a magickal being by nature, I must not forget to take pause for the human experience. Which is fancy jargon for, slow down and live within the moment; don't tie yourself to more than your soul can carry. Yes, we are strengthened by that which takes us outside of our comfort zones and seeks to progressively add more weight to our sedentary lives. However, we must remain cognizant that sometimes too much weight does nothing more than break all that it encounters. Therefore, we must remember that in order to get stronger, we must sync our steps with our thoughts and take things one at a time. ♥

*Journal Entry: "Moving Ahead"*

Last night I had a beautiful dream. It wasn't elaborate, and I didn't even know the people in it, but it was the feeling it invoked that made it so beautiful. I had the overwhelming feeling I was on task and exactly where I needed to be. I am now realizing that in order to be in the right place, at the right time, I must accept the good with the bad, or at least my perceptions of such things. Darkness may try to combat my progress or even set up false shortcuts, but I will remain on the course that was predestined for my existence.

Our fates were written in the stars long before even our ancestors walked the Earth. It is up to us to focus in order to remain on track because there will always be something or someone that, either knowingly or unknowingly, attempts to detour our journey. Acknowledge your roadblocks just long enough to navigate around them. Embrace your destiny with love, light and truth in your heart. Vow to make today the greatest day yet. ♥

~*~*~*~

## What does it all mean?

There will always be moments that serve as potential obstructions towards your efforts to be the change you wish to see during this journey called life. The key is not to pretend they don't exist. Instead, you must acknowledge them for what they are, whether it is something internal or external to your being. This could come in the form of a relationship that is not healthy for your growth, or even just a way of thinking that works to pull you back into a dark mindset. The shadow exists within each of us. To deny it is to deny self. Instead, recognize your many facets, but don't allow the darkness to seduce you into the days of old.

Chapter XII: THE SEDUCTION

LURED BY DARKNESS

I can remember entering into a mall by myself, a mall I had never been. I entered through the main department store that served as anchor for the south end. Then, I quickly noticed that it was like a maze as there seemed to be so much going on with the store being under construction. The employees were forcing all the customers to leave, which created an even more chaotic scene. As I was exiting the store, I noticed it was leading me to the entrance of a bazaar. I was impressed with its Mediterranean vibe. It was different to what I was accustomed to, yet, I remember feeling so excited to see the new things. There were so many vibrant hues that had a richness seemingly coming from the source of color in and of itself. The shops, the vendors, all were working separately but flowing as if it were a show in which the most extravagant display was to win a great prize. There were games and the art… the art was breathtaking. Ornate mosaics that would leave the most talented artist in awe and admiration, simply put, it was beautiful. Then, I noticed there was a strange trend to this place. It reminded me of Mardi Gras and was presented almost as if it were held by a circus. There were belly dancers that charmed snakes and barbers that could cut their clients' hair perfectly while blindfolded! It was a party for the senses! However, I could sense that there was something wicked about this place. I felt it was demon possessed and, therefore, had the strong urge to leave.

I attempted to abscond from the bazaar but seemed to only wander in circles. The once joyful and alluring event had now turned into a labyrinth of darkness that had no intention of letting me escape. My instincts told me to head for the art shop where I had admired the mosaics. It seemed to be the calmest place amongst the mass of shops. I made my way there, entering the store. All the while, I could feel eyes watching my every move. There was someone or something in the back room, the very room towards which I found myself approaching. My soul instantly saw that which my eyes had not yet seen: it was a demon of ill intent. He was obsessed with me and had decided he wanted me for his own and would do anything to lure me into joining him and forever walking by his side. I was to be his bride. There was no amount of money or extravagance that would be spared to seduce me into his lair.

## Behind the Story

Truth be told, darkness can have a certain appeal. It can call to all senses. It can read your desires and pretend to offer fulfillment. However, just as with an emotionless seduction, the heat dissipates after the moment has passed. Ultimately, you are more often than not left with an even greater void than whence you began. I understand the attraction. I can empathize with the allure. I often find myself being called back to former ways of destruction and self-doubt. I hear the whispers in my ear that tell me I should throw in the "love and light towel" and resort to the simplicity of not caring. Climb back into the comfort of darkness, because at least then I wouldn't have to put forth any effort. Trust me, I understand. It is a natural part of the process of change.

We must realize that the natural state of being isn't to dwell in darkness, confusion and self depreciating behavior. No, these are things that we learned along the way, "growing up", regardless of where the lessons originate. This is the actual work, folks! It takes work to foster feelings of negativity and resentment. No one is born with hate in their heart… Perhaps it's time that we remember what we've long taught ourselves to forget.

Journal Entry: "Overruled"

Some days seem as if I truly can't catch a break! I am awakened with a jolt, handed a cluster of frustration followed by a bag full of emotional irritation. I think to myself, "What else?" What else? Hmm...I suppose I ask and I shall receive, because no sooner does the thought cross my mind before I realize I'm continuing down the path of perceived sorrow, frustration and disappointment.

Perhaps I'm going about this bad day notion all wrong. Perhaps by feeding into my anxieties and disappointments I am giving them the nourishment they need to remain strong. Perhaps I am actually exacerbating the problems instead of looking for the silver lining in whatever I might be experiencing at the moment. Sure this is much easier said than done, but as I've mentioned before, if something is easy, it is rarely worth much.

Yes, I am human and yes, I make mistakes. However, I am working on becoming the best me that I can be for the sake of self and then for the sake of the greater picture. So today, I try not to be overruled by the darkness that the enemy is constantly trying to drive into my core. Instead, in moments of despair I will continue to reach for HIS hand to pull me through. After all, HE wouldn't give me the weight if HE felt I couldn't carry it.

*Never leave me nor forsake me!* :)

==Remember, when you are in darkness, simply look for light. It will always lead you the right way.== ♥

## Journal Entry: "Invisible Attacks"

I had a vision that I kept being attacked by some sort of invisible force. This force lurked everywhere I was and everywhere I was going to be. It only wanted to inflict harm and pain on me, regardless of how good I was; perhaps even *despite* how much love and light I held in my heart and actions. It persisted in coming for me in spite of my attempts to avoid attack.

First, it cut my legs from under me. So, I got prosthetics. Then, it ripped my heart from my chest. So, I got a replacement. It then turned on those that I held closest to my heart. Consequently, I placed them in a bubble of love and protection so that no harm could befall them. Yet, through all my efforts to counter the attacks, it remained diligent in its charge to take my soul.

You see, this isn't about avoiding conflict when it is brought to your door. It's about you, and you alone being in charge of whether you choose to react or respond. When darkness knocks on your door, as it will, you must remember to lock the deadbolt. If it still sneaks in, don't ask if it would like a cup of tea. I realize it can often be exhausting to live in a suit of armor, constantly battling darkness and standing for what you feel is right. Yet, in these moments, we are not victims. We are called to be soldiers in an army of greatness, called to the frontlines to ensure the perpetuity of all that we hold dear.

There is always hope when we take responsibility for ourselves and act accordingly. ♥

*Journal Entry: "Rejection"*

I've watched all the interviews where "famous people" comment on how they were rejected a million times before they got their *big break*, but I always seemed so removed from this notion. In reality, I've never felt the true sting of rejection, with one exception and even that exception, turned into a magnificent ending. So, why in the world am I writing on a subject I admittedly know so little about? Great question!

Truth is, I am not familiar with rejection because I simply see it as redirection. You know the saying "When one door closes, another one opens"? Well, that has truly been my life's experience. It is how I choose to see the moments that could be perceived to an outsider as rejection. Instead of harping and dwelling, I embrace the fact that by being told *no*, I didn't end up spinning my wheels just to remain in a stationary position.

I will continue to listen beyond the silence that beckons for depression by whispering dark notions of defeat, and recognize them as moments of triumph. I will push forward and persist through the suggestions that attempt to play on lowering my self-esteem and enhancing my insecurities. The only true rejection or failure resides in that which we create for ourselves. If we choose to give-up, then and <u>only</u> then, do we accept defeat. ♥

*Journal Entry: "Demons"*

When my daughter tells me that she sees a monster, I tell her the following: "You tell that monster to go away! Let him know that he isn't welcome in our home and that he has to leave!"

I lead with this because everyone has faced their proverbial monsters and has suffered their fair share of demons. Some more extreme than others, but we all have them no less. They manifest themselves in the form of haunting memories of a perceived negative situation from the past or present.

In reality most demons are given strength by us. We breathe life into their existence, either knowingly or not, by constantly talking about them or by not working to overcome their perceived importance in our lives. Think of it this way, a car is just a hunk of metal until we give it gas (or plug it in… good ole modern technology). Well, the same can be said of demons. If we are able to release the thoughts, memories or insecurities that are associated with granting importance to these dark moments, we in effect take the gas out of the car (or demon).

The moment we stop seeking that verbal or silent apology for what we see as being done to us, is the moment we regain our power. We must recognize that although we don't and can't control many situations, we are not victims. I recognize that, again, this is not the simplest thing to do; to stop feeding into something we have spent our lives defending on a subconscious level. To not always need to respond to the things being said to you, and instead walk away with head high, dignity in tact, respect shown and acceptance of coexistence. Even more so, the actions of the past do in fact play a major role in shaping our realities of today. However, we do not need to continuously grant power to the negative influence. Instead claim we should claim our own power to overcome with strength and love.

The journey of change requires diligence and conscious effort. So, let us collectively take away the enemy's power by choosing to rise above anything that could even dream of bringing us down. Focus on being righteous and not just right. Let go of your demons.

♥

*Journal Entry: "Embracing the Shadows"*

Ok, so now that we've let go of the demons, we must address the things that we can never outrun: our shadows.

Ever have the feeling as if your life were progressing in the usual forward motion, while your dreams are pulling you backwards? For instance, my life is filled with blessings (which I count daily), but it also has its fair share of ups-and-downs. Plus, lately it seems as if for all the love and light I try to emit in my waking life, my slumber attempts to put me in a holding pattern. It's as if I experience an alternate reality while I sleep, one that has me often playing the lead along with several co-starring characters at once. Most of the time, I am completely aware that I am dreaming and have control over my actions. I can even go as far as to tell myself to look for key markers (time, location, emotions, small details, etc). I must admit that it leaves me quite exhausted in my waking life because I often feel as if I have never truly rested. But, the lucid dreams and out of body experiences are not what I wish to focus on for the sake of this entry.

This other world seems to cast light onto the actions of my past. It regenerates moments that have brought me to where I am today through actions that are not necessarily *fitting* or in-line with whom most people think me to be. This world reminds me of where I have come from, and not only aims to keep me grounded, but it serves to oftentimes exhume my past decisions. I equate this to a night of excessive drinking replayed over-and-over as if it were on a constant loop, forcing me to relive some of my darkest moments.

However, as with all things, if I am to continue successfully on this journey, I must cast aside my gag-reflex and delve into what I am being shown if I wish to learn my life's lessons. I must in-turn ask myself:

- What emotions does this dream state stir within?
- Why are these emotions so raw?
- Have I not faced this former reality, and am therefore being held in loop until I truly address the past?

The ironic part of it all is that I have always been the person to play the *hard* role. I have never really been the type to be affected by much outside of myself, let alone being affected by anything internal. I generally get over things quickly, and to the outside eye, this is done quite effortlessly. I manage the role of unbreakable soldier while harboring the sensitivities of the entire world within my heart. I am learning now to merge the worlds that exist within so I may better serve the collective. Yet, that leaves such issues as addressing the darkness within my being, whether it is the shadows of my past or the moments as they occur in my present.

I understand that we all have parts of ourselves that we would rather dismiss or force into the shadows. However, if we are to successfully manage the tightrope of our true selves, we must not pretend that this dark side of us doesn't exist. Instead, we must embrace these shadows for what and who they are. Dive into the shadows in order to truly understand the workings of self. After all, we can never rise into our true promise and power if we leave a major part of our souls in the past.

Don't forget to explore your shadows because we can only run from them so long. Eventually, we are forced to stop and catch our breath. Remember, we cannot be seduced into darkness if we see it coming from a mile away. ♥

~*~*~*~

*What does it all mean?*

The shadows, the darkness, the seduction, they are all a part of this journey. We are not perfect beings, but that doesn't give us just cause to not strive for greatness. We must seek within and truly embrace all facets of self in order to remain successful on this journey to change. Will you have hiccups along the way? Of course! At times, the allure of the darkness will seem so sexy you have to silence all temptations. But this journey is so much bigger than those temptations. Think about the bigger picture! Why do you want to make a change in your life? Are you happy with the world the way it is?

In those instances of temptation, take a second to consider how far you've come and in that moment embrace the fact that you can continue on.

## Chapter XIII: HOW FAR WE'VE COME

### A GLANCE OVER THE SHOULDER

Thanks to the modern conveniences that exist to help us keep in touch with one another, I still have a reference of where I was when I first joined the social media frenzy. My perceptions, thought processes, even my reality all sit in silence, waiting to be beckoned to the forefront for means of exploration. No, I don't have need to look into my past to see how far I've come. Rather, I see this as an opportunity for greater clarity on the person I stand as today.

Have you ever looked into your high school yearbook and thought, "What was I thinking?!" Or had a laugh with friends as you reminisced over days of old? Well, these are all ways of checking your points of reference. This does not mean that you must remain in the past or even consider those memories as the best days of your life. Instead, you should look at it as an opportunity to review your growth chart and to recognize that if you were able to grow from that past, you can continue to grow into the future. And on the contrary, if you look back and see that you are still in the same place doing the same things, and this state of being does not serve your advancement in becoming the change you wish to see, then grasp this opportunity to take control over where you choose to go from here.

My past is nowhere near spotless. As I've mentioned at the start of this book, my former views of the world around me were quite skewed towards the direction of cynicism and negativity. Yet, change can happen in a split second if we are open to it. The events that made me decide to proceed towards love and light were that of tragedy and loss. I knew that something needed to give in order for me to secure a better future for myself and my family. There was no longer the luxury of pretending to be unaffected by local and global milestones that reflected the world's downward spiral.

The truth is, change is not an option. It is a necessity. In order for us to truly become the change we wish to see in the world, we must first look inward to address that which aims to hinder our personal progress. Again, your journey will not mirror mine and that is completely ok. You will have bumps in the road and you will even have moments of regression. This path is not about lingering on the wrongs, but focusing on what's right.

If you are just as tired as I am of living in the war zone we as individuals have built through complacency and division amongst the masses, then do something about it! We do not need to take up arms in order to unmask that which aims to shield our internal light. We simply need to stand as beacons; those that are willing, ready and able will be drawn to your light and reflect in kind.

There is no lesson to be mentioned here because at this point you ARE the lesson. Live your life according to love, respect and understanding. You may not agree with everyone, but you can learn to co-exist. This is not about trends, fashion or even political agenda. This is about making the world a better place, period.

Now, I ask YOU, are you ready to…

*Begin YOUR Journey?*

Marisa Moments

Start your own journal now →

## Journal Entry:

Now that you've read about some of my stops along the journey in this thing called life, take a moment to write down some of your own moments. It's a great means of self-reflection and realization. Go ahead; write anything your heart desires. Give it a try!

Made in the USA
Charleston, SC
07 August 2014